P9-DOA-430

BELLE MORAL
A Natural History

by

Ann-Marie MacDonald

with an introductory essay by
Kathleen Gallagher
and an Afterword by the author

Shaw
The Academy of the Shaw Festival

PLAYWRIGHTS CANADA PRESS

ST.THOMAS PUBLIC LIBRARY

JUN - - 2006

Library and Archives Canada Cataloguing in Publication
MacDonald, Ann-Marie
  Belle Moral : a natural history / by Ann-Marie MacDonald ; with an introductory essay by Kathleen Gallagher and an afterword by the author.
A play.
ISBN 0-9699478-7-9 (Academy of the Shaw Festival).—
ISBN 0-88754-824-5 (Playwrights Canada Press)
  I. Academy of the Shaw Festival II. Title.
PS8575.D38B45 2005   C812'.54   C2005-903926-4

Co-published in 2005 by
The Academy of the Shaw Festival
P.O. Box 774, Niagara-on-the-Lake, Ontario L0S 1J0
www.shawfest.com

and

Playwrights Canada Press
215 Spadina Avenue, Suite 230, Toronto, Ontario M5T 2C7
www.playwrightscanada.com
Orders from orders@playwrightscanada.com

Copyright © 2005 Ann-Marie MacDonald. CAUTION: This play is fully protected under the copyright laws of Canada and all other countries of The Copyright Union, and is subject to royalty. Changes to the script are expressly forbidden without the prior written permission of the author. Rights to produce, film, or record, in whole or in part, in any medium or any language, by any group, amateur of professional, are retained by the author. For production rights, contact Lorraine Wells at 416-413-1676.

No part of this book, covered by the copyright hereon, may be reproduced or used in any form or by any means – graphic, electronic or mechanical – without the prior written permission of the publisher except for excerpts in a review. Any request for photocopying, recording, taping or information storage and retrieval systems of any part of this book shall be directed in writing to Access Copyright, 1 Yonge Street, Suite 1900, Toronto, Ontario Canada M5E 1E5 416-868-1620.

Financial support provided by the taxpayers of Canada and Ontario through the Canada Council for the Arts, and the Department of Canadian Heritage through the Book Publishing Industry Development Programme, and the Ontario Arts Council.

Edited by Denis Johnston and Jean German
Page layout by Jean German, cover design by Scott McKowen
Printed and bound by Canadian Printco Ltd. at Toronto, Canada
Author photo by Gabor Jurina

La Fin de Siècle and the Pull of Opposites

by Kathleen Gallagher

"What is objectivity but the ability to consider every influence on our powers of observation? Facts, uprooted, can tell us only so much. A fact out of context is like a fish on a slab, inexplicable without water." And so it is *the story*, an "inextricable web of affinities," said Darwin, and not disembodied facts, that Ann-Marie MacDonald draws us into. In our journey to the coast of Scotland, 1899, she asks us to remember our own childhoods, our dreams and ghosts and hauntings, our apprehension of a world that calls on all of our senses. She asks us to *observe* our lives, our part in evolution. "We are all here so briefly," says Pearl. "Awake, for a moment. Unique, for a moment. Able to look and to love, for a moment."

Theatre, unlike literature, is a social art form and so it is important that we are here together to participate – to see, hear, smell the stories percolating deep inside the stone walls, hidden attic, and candle-lit drawing room of Belle Moral. Five miles outside Edinburgh, itself a haunted city with phantom pipers and memories of murder, we are thrust into the present lives and troubling histories of the MacIsaac family.

Everywhere we turn, there is the pull of opposites: science versus nature, rational versus supernatural, past and present, conscious and unconscious, public and private, truths and lies, Protestant and Catholic, normal or deviant, highland versus lowland, drunk or abstemious, French or English, masculine and feminine, tragedy and comedy. *Belle Moral* is, in some ways, a meditation on these and other great themes of human preoccupation.

Historically, Scotland has been a place of just such contradictions. It is a land of legends, first whispered by fairies: crashing waves of the North Sea, twisting roads lined with stone, mist-covered mountains and sounds of distant pipes, flutes, harps, and wailing banshees; stories of monsters who live alongside the mortals that inhabit the small country. And in this world of fairies and hideous creatures, we have science's search for truth. After the last battle for its independence from English rule in the spring of 1746, the undaunted spirit, the pride and deep curiosity of a people earned Scotland and the Scottish Enlightenment its glorious reputation in the story of the modern world and its advancement of human understanding. A recent book, *How the Scots Invented the Modern World* (2001), even argues that the great Scottish scientists and inventors of the second half of the nineteenth century – Watt, Telford, Nasmyth –

INTRODUCTION

were largely responsible for the building and organization of the British empire.

Beneath the rugged beauty of the coast and Scotland's scientific genesis, we have the story of Pearl MacIsaac, a budding scientist in her own right. The biological determinism and moralism of social Darwinism, however, saw the emancipation of women as an attack on patriarchal culture and the "natural" way of the world. These rebellious daughters were swiftly labelled mentally disturbed or suffering from "nerves". In her book *The Female Malady* (1985), Elaine Showalter points out that Jean-Martin Charcot, one of the first European theorists of the female disease that came to be known as hysteria, believed that hysterics suffered from a hereditary taint that weakened the nervous system. The ovarian region, he concluded, was a particularly sensitive "hysterogenic zone". In addition, he developed a theory suggesting that hysteria also had psychological origins. As such theories of biological sexual difference were given full scientific weight, the Victorian ideals of femininity tightened their grip.

Sigmund Freud, however, began to recognize the social and cultural constraints on women, and with his colleague Josef Breuer produced their *Studies on Hysteria* in 1895. This work presented a much more sympathetic view, maintaining that hysterics were not insane, but "people of the clearest intellect, strongest will, greatest character, and highest critical power". Freud and Breuer's case

studies stood in contrast to many of the hostile por-
traits of hysterical females presented by European
physicians of the Victorian period. At Belle Moral,
however, it is brother Victor's lust for life that most
effectively unsettles the gender codes. "Victor is
morbidly effeminate," claims Pearl, but Victor is
the artist, the female subject position, and not the
effeminate. He is the one who seduces us into the
struggle against repression. "The artist is the one
who refuses initiation through education into the
existing order," offered Norman O. Brown in a 1959
study of Freud's work. Hence the dialectical inter-
play, in the play, between the extreme Rationalism of Dr Reid, who believes that insanity can be
avoided by a life of moderation and the exercise of
the will, and the ideals of those like Victor the Romantic, more drawn to the willing suspension of
common sense.

While "lunatics" of the *fin de siècle* often fell
silent or succumbed to paralytic seizures, Victor
concocts a rich dream-life as an outlet for his spirit
and a clear, sobering philosophy by which to live.
Dreams, or wish-fulfillment, are the work of the
unconscious, argued Freud, at a time when his con-
temporaries had little appreciation for such things
that could not be properly measured. Both Pearl
and Victor are immersed in the life of the imagination, which opens up other worlds. These "other
worlds," it might be said, underlie our "normal"
experience, and for both Pearl and Victor there is
a dangerous yet desirable attraction to the irration-

al, the seemingly abnormal. Playwright MacDonald believes that "consciousness and dreams form a compound as necessary for life as hydrogen and oxygen."

If Freud was right in suggesting that our dreams, our humour, and slips of the tongue explain in some way our mental states, and reveal in covert form what would otherwise not be understood at all, Pearl may well be on the cusp of discovering what was always there, morally inescapable but unarticulated: Darwin's "inextricable web of affinities". While Dr Reid might be playing God with his presumptuous science, Pearl's love illuminates the important questions: "And what are we to do in God's place? How are we to know what God's work is?"

Ann-Marie MacDonald has been interested in alchemical transformations, the unconscious, and the fantasies of gender play since such earlier works as *Goodnight Desdemona (Good Morning Juliet)* and *Anything That Moves*. These are narrative interests we have seen before. But in *Belle Moral*, the world of the senses and sense perception also drive these narrative tropes. We have Auntie Flora who believes in the communication of spirits ("Your ancestors are tryin' to tell you something") and Puppy with the canine sense, more acute than that of humans and more sensitive to the supernatural presence.

But what or who will be transformed this time? How does history get mapped onto the present? Where might our unconscious lead us in our pursuits of truth? How do our ancestors talk to us? Do we admit to our connection in diversity, to our common ancestry, to being a part of that "exquisitely, well-nigh infinitely complex web?" Darwin himself explained:

> Analogy would lead me one step further, namely, to the belief that all animals and plants have descended from some one prototype...Therefore, I should infer from analogy that probably all the organic beings which have ever lived on this earth, have descended from some one primordial form, into which life was first breathed.

Perhaps it is no surprise that Ann-Marie Mac-Donald would tell a truly postmodern tale set at the height of the great project of modernity, for paradox is her centerpiece, while story is her form:

> PEARL. Doctor, you look at us and see a jumble of unrelated, distasteful facts. I look and see affinities.
> VICTOR. A story.
> PEARL. That's right. A plot.

Deeply implicated in our own histories of family and culture, MacDonald takes the socially "natural" configuration of family and paradoxically asks how sure we can ever be of the constitution of family. If it is the case that "we are free agents as well as products of history, accidental and inevitable, like the best stories," then family can be imagined and can further set our psychic apparatus in motion, as in a wish. Our roots/routes to family are multiple.

Pulled, as always, by the reconciliation of opposites, Ann-Marie MacDonald has an unquenchable fascination with puzzles and a certain penchant for the comic turn:

> PEARL. I don't believe in ghosts.
>
> FLORA. That's of nay concern to the ghosts.

Seeking to regain the lost laughter of childhood, she can rarely resist a pun or the opportunity to find the playful in the serious, especially, she explains, when she writes for the theatre. In an interview published in 2003, MacDonald describes what she does as driven by a "love of the audience" and a "love of performing:"

> I found a great intellectual hunger and curiosity, combined with a love of stories and a love of the fabulous... I want to give the audience a reason to stay, give them a reason to want to find out more and to want to identify with different points of view, different experiences. For me, that's my hardcore passion: put yourself in someone else's shoes.

As we move into the final scenes of *Belle Moral*, MacDonald's love of the fabulous is in full force; the secrets, laid bare. For lies never protect us, as poor Dr Reid must learn. "Knowledge is power," said Sir Francis Bacon in the sixteenth century, and this became a slogan of the Enlightenment midway between his time and our own. Since then, the closet doors have burst open... *tant mieux*! We need to know our stories and let the ghosts out.

Kathleen Gallagher is Associate Professor and holds a Canada Research Chair at the Ontario Institute for Studies in Education, University of Toronto (OISE/UT). She has published many articles on drama, education, and the sociology of arts, and her book Drama Education in the Lives of Girls: Imagining Possibilities *(2000) received the American Education Research Association's book award for significant contribution to Curriculum Studies. Her edited collection* How Theatre Educates: Convergences and Counterpoints with Artists, Scholars, and Advocates, *(2003) argues for a broader understanding and definition of theatre as an educative force.*

BELLE MORAL
A Natural History

For Zsa Zsa

BELLE MORAL

A Natural History

Dramatis Personae

THE BRIDE

THE JACKAL

PEARL MACISAAC,
   thirty-two, an amateur scientist

FLORA MACISAAC,
   a lady in her late fifties / early sixties

VICTOR MACISAAC,
   Pearl's younger brother, twenty-seven

YOUNG FARLEIGH, an elderly servant

DR SEAMUS REID,
   a gentleman in his late fifties /
   early sixties

PUPPY,
   a black dog with a flat head for patting

MR ABBOTT, a solicitor in his thirties

WEE FARLEIGH,
   a young and handsome servant

THE CREATURE

CLAIRE, a young woman

*The action takes place in spring and summer
1899 on the coast of Scotland, a few miles outside Edinburgh, in a large old stone house called Belle Moral.*

The Arab's Mouth, an earlier version of this play, premiered at the Factory Theatre, Toronto, in the fall of 1990, with the following cast:

Pearl	MARTHA BURNS
Ramsay / Anubis / Mr Abbott	DEREK BOYES
Victor	HENRY CZERNY
Dr Reid	DAVID FOX
Flora	PATRICIA HAMILTON
Nun / Puppy / Creature	MARTHA ROSS

Directed by MAUREEN WHITE

Designed by SUE LePAGE

Lighting designed by LESLIE WILKINSON

Sound designed by DAVID AKAL JAGGS

Dramaturgy by MAUREEN WHITE
and JACKIE MAXWELL

Stage Manager: MARIA POPOFF

Assistant Director: DEREK BOYES

(The role of Mr Abbott
was cut in subsequent revisions.)

Belle Moral: A Natural History was first performed at the Shaw Festival Theatre, Niagara-on-the-Lake, on July 7, 2005, with the following cast:

Pearl MacIsaac	FIONA BYRNE
Flora MacIsaac	DONNA BELLEVILLE
Victor MacIsaac	JEFF MEADOWS
Young Farleigh	BERNARD BEHRENS
Dr Seamus Reid	PETER MILLARD
The Jackal / Wee Farleigh	JEFF MADDEN
The Bride / Creature / Claire	JESSICA LOWRY
Mr Abbott	GRAEME SOMERVILLE

Directed by ALISA PALMER
Designed by JUDITH BOWDEN
Lighting designed by KEVIN LAMOTTE
Original music composed by PAUL SPORTELLI

Stage management by
Joanna Jurychuk and Christine Oakey

*The Playwright would like to extend
her thanks to Paul Birt, Jerry Doiron,
Margaret Gaffney, Jean German, Denis Johnston,
John Hugh MacDonald, Jackie Maxwell,
Nadine McInnis, Alisa Palmer and Maureen White.*

ACT I

Scene 1 The Underworld

Night. Sound of the sea. A BRIDE *enters, dressed in a flowing white gown, and veil that covers her face. She is searching for something by the light of her candle. Delicate distant melody, "Au Claire de la Lune". In one corner, lies a faded tartan blanket; sound of an infant crying.* THE BRIDE *is drawn toward the blanket. Sound of a bagpipe drone.* THE BRIDE *picks up the blanket, then pauses, sensing the presence behind her: it is a man with the head of a jackal reminiscent of Anubis. There is a formality to his movements. He is neither malevolent nor benevolent, merely a guide, a conductor of souls to the underworld. He claims the blanket from* THE BRIDE, *and blows out her candle. Ambient female cry, "Pearl!"*

Scene 2 Pearl's Study at Belle Moral

Night. PEARL *is sitting bolt upright at her desk, eyes wide, having just awakened from the nightmare. She is dressed in high-collar blouse and neatly tailored tweeds. Her study is a model of Victorian polymathic precision: books, fossils, butterfly case, skulls of various species, a telescope, a microscope. Her desk is littered with papers and in one corner of it sits a murky specimen jar. A knocking at the door.* PEARL *blinks.*

19

FLORA [*offstage*]. Pearl?

> FLORA MACISAAC *enters with a lamp, a set of keys at her waist.*

PEARL. Auntie Flora?

FLORA. Were you ridin' the nightmare again, pet?

PEARL [*business-like*]. Perhaps I was. I don't remember.

FLORA. You must endeavour to remember, dear. Your ancestors are tryin' to tell you something.

PEARL. Which ancestors are those, Auntie? The apes or the amoebas?

FLORA. Do go to bed, pet, it's nigh on three.

PEARL. I can't, Auntie, I'm working. [*crisp and efficient*] I intend to submit an article on Cretaceous Caledonian mollusks to the Royal Geological Society in London, and this time I shall sign it, "Percival MacIsaac, Esquire". See if they dismiss "Percy" with the same alacrity with which they advised "Pearl" to return to more womanly pursuits.

FLORA. What in the Lord's name is that?

PEARL. The Cretaceous Period, Auntie, a fossil-rich –

FLORA. No, dear. That.

ACT I

PEARL. Oh, that [*picking up the specimen jar*]. It is the tufted ear of a clinical idiot, upon which there is a point. Marvelous, isn't it? Observe the whorls, the delicate lobe, at once so familiar, so... human; jarringly juxtaposed with the unmistakeable bestial peak into which the top of the ear resolves. And the thick growth of what could never be described as mere hair. See? Still glossy, gracefully suspended in sterile solution: fur.

FLORA. Wherever did you obtain such a blasphemy?

PEARL. Dr Reid...

FLORA. Dr Reid?

PEARL. Yes. He very kindly loaned it me when I admired it on the shelf of his laboratory. Dr Reid was quite the budding Darwin in his day, did you know that, Auntie? A pity, he abandoned his research. And what a shame, a specimen like this gathering dust.

FLORA. Dr Reid's got no business lending you that ear.

PEARL. Why ever not?

    A beat.

FLORA. It's... *rhuadh*. [pron: roo-ah]

PEARL. It's what? Speak English, Auntie.

FLORA. It's red.

PEARL. So?

FLORA. That's Faery hair.

PEARL. Auntie, I'm a redhead, Father was a redhead, are we fairies?

FLORA. No, no, dear, but...

PEARL. But what?

FLORA. You might have a gift.

PEARL. And what's wrong with that?

FLORA. The gifts of the Faery can be... queer.

PEARL. Well this ear is certainly a gift, if not of "the Faery", then of Nature.

FLORA. Nature makes mistakes. And tisna' wise to gaze too long upon them. You might look at something and find you can never look away again.

> PEARL *peers at the jar through her magnifying glass.*

The evil eye dwells in that which is unnatural. Just say a little prayer and put it down, there's a good lass.

PEARL. Make up your mind, Auntie, are you Pagan or Protestant, you can't be both you know. Or rather you can, in which case you're Catholic.

ACT I

FLORA [*scandalized*]. I'm no' Catholic – !

PEARL. I shall contemplate this ear to my heart's content, for it is an aberration; one of Nature's exceptions by which we divine Her rules.

FLORA. Look to your own ears, my dear. Thank God He shaped you in His image and do not dwell upon the margin He left to the divil.

PEARL. Auntie Flora, the "divil's margin" is merely a necessary factor of chance by which all life on Earth has evolved.

FLORA. There's that evil word again.

PEARL. There's nothing evil about evolution, Auntie; it's just a lot of hit and miss in the struggle for reproductive success.

FLORA. Pearl... isn't there any young man you think of more than another?

PEARL. In what sense?

FLORA. Have you heard from Mr Abbott lately?

PEARL. I should think Mr Abbott is waiting to hear from us. He can't very well read Father's will with half the family still off gallivanting.

FLORA. I meant, have you heard from him... socially?

PEARL [*suddenly*]. Auntie. I dreamt I was wearing Mother's wedding gown.

FLORA [*delighted*]. Ach, did you, lass, and were you by chance able to glimpse the groom?

PEARL. Auntie Flora, I'm going to buy a dog.

FLORA. What? Oh no, pet, now don't you go buyin' a dog.

PEARL. Why not?

FLORA. Why... your father could never abide a slaverin' cur.

PEARL. I shall select a non-slavering breed. Besides. Father is dead. And the dog is for Victor. Why are you dressed?

FLORA. I was waiting up... [*prevaricating*] in case your brother should arrive. His letter said today.

PEARL. And the letter before that said last week. I'd not lose sleep over Victor, Auntie, he'll turn up when he pleases, in three days or three months. Depending on who's standing him drinks.

FLORA. Don't worry, pet.

PEARL. I'm not worried, I'm vexed.

FLORA. You're hungry.

PEARL. Peckish.

ACT I

FLORA. What about a nice pickled egg? Or, Young Farleigh's fixed a lovely finan haddie.

PEARL. Any herring?

FLORA. There's bloater paste. And a dollop of marmite on toast.

PEARL. Mmmm.

FLORA. I'll go heap a plate. Now you get back to your stones and snails and puppy-dog tails and... forget about that ear. Especially at this hour.

PEARL. What hour is that, Auntie? "The hour of the Faery"?

FLORA. The hour of the wolf.

Sound of carriage wheels on gravel.

PEARL. Ha! The prodigal returns [*rising, delighted in spite of herself*]. Let's have a right midnight feast with silly old Victor, shall we Auntie?

FLORA [*urgent*]. Stay, Pearl! [*covering*] It mightn't be him.

PEARL. Well who might it be "at this hour"?

FLORA [*thinking quickly*]. Young Farleigh.

PEARL. Young Farleigh? What's he doing out about?

FLORA. I sent him down to the shore for winkles.

PEARL. Ugh, I can't abide winkles.

FLORA. Your brother loves them.

PEARL. He can have them [*sitting*]. Along with everything else.

FLORA. Hush now, this will a'ways be your haim. Our haim.

PEARL. Don't console me, Auntie, I am quite steeled to my fate. In fact I relish the prospect of Victor inheriting Belle Moral with all its cash and chattels, and squandering the lot within a year. I shall then be forced to earn my living. Book a passage to Egypt. Cross the desert on a camel. Publish my findings anonymously. Return in glory.

FLORA [*going to exit*]. I'll fetch some cocoa too.

PEARL. Auntie Flora... was Father proud of me?

FLORA. Ach, you know he was. Look at you. Educated. Modern. And not a bit dried out.

PEARL. I've had the oddest feeling lately. Ever since Father's funeral. As if there was someone missing. But I can't say who. I suppose you'd say my ancestors are trying to tell me something.

   A beat.

FLORA. You miss your father. That's all it is.

PEARL. Poor Victor always wanted a puppy.

ACT I

A clock strikes three. FLORA *exits.* PEARL *resumes her work.*

Scene 3 The Driveway

FLORA *stands outside Belle Moral, holding a lantern, peering into the darkness toward the sound of a horse exhaling, pawing the gravel. A carriage door opens. A footfall.* FLORA *sees the new arrival. She makes the sign of the cross.*

Scene 4 The Drawing Room

Next morning. Over the mantelpiece hangs a family portrait. It is painted in the impressionist style with the prettiness of Monet and the fogginess of Turner. The figures are distinguishable as a bearded red-haired man, a dark-haired woman cradling an infant in a tartan shawl, and PEARL *as a young child. There is a sense of the portrait being compositionally off-balance: a gap between* PEARL *and the infant. On the opposite wall is mounted a set of bagpipes of the same tartan.* PEARL *is huddled under the hood of a camera.* FLORA *stands posed, draped in a white bedsheet.*

FLORA. Is it to be a religious theme this time, pet?

PEARL. In a manner of speaking. Classical mythology.

FLORA. I'll no' be a pagan, Pearl.

PEARL. It's purely symbolic, Auntie [*handing her scissors and a ball of yarn*]. You're one of the Fates.

FLORA. What am I knitting?

PEARL. You're capriciously toying with the life of some poor sod.

FLORA. Aren't there any nice myth women?

PEARL. No. None of any importance.

> FLORA *strikes a pose, scissors poised to cut a length of yarn.*

Don't smile, Auntie.

FLORA. Well how do you want me?

PEARL. Dispassionate. This is a scientific journal. Hold still, now.

> PEARL *goes to the take the picture but* FLORA *cocks an ear.*

What is it?

FLORA. Nowt. Thought I heard something.

PEARL [*about to take the picture again*]. Ready? And –

> FLORA *cocks an ear again.*

You're not going dafty on me now, are you, Auntie?

ACT I

FLORA. No, dear, I'm a touch forfochen this morning is all.

PEARL [*matter-of-fact*]. Up half the night worrying about Victor, damn him, you look dreadful. Ready now? One, two, three —

> VICTOR *enters, wearing a kilt, causing* FLORA *to smile the instant* PEARL *takes the picture with a poof and a flash.*

FLORA. Victor!

VICTOR [*to* FLORA, *playfully passionate*]. My God, what Attic vision; what vestal beauty stands here poised to cut or to extend a mortal skein? Fly, maiden, and transform thyself into a tree, else must I taste thine antique fruits, for I am the Highland Pan!

> *They hug.* FLORA *embraces him fervently.*

FLORA. Victor, ma bonnie, you should have let us know, we'd've sent Young Farleigh with the cart.

VICTOR. Hello, Pearl.

> *He opens his arms, beaming, but she does not embrace him.*

PEARL [*arch*]. What are you doing, gadding about in that savage raiment?

VICTOR. Airing my privates.

PEARL. Don't be disgusting.

Rapidly.

VICTOR. Don't start.

PEARL. You started it.

VICTOR. I did not.

PEARL. Indeed you did.

VICTOR. A didna.

PEARL. Did.

VICTOR. Didna.

PEARL. Did.

VICTOR. Didna – !   PEARL. Dididid – !

FLORA [*making peace*]. Noo where's yer fit bin gangin' this time, laddie? London? Paris? Rome?

VICTOR. Glasgow.

PEARL [*dismissive*]. Ha.

VICTOR. I was looking to trace Mother's ancestors.

PEARL. And what did you discover swinging from the family tree? A backward lot of Highland crofters with an unwholesome fondness for things *Fr-r-rench*; blood-thirsty and Catholic to boot.

VICTOR [*grand*]. A martyred race: soaked in glory, culture –

ACT I

PEARL. And whiskey.

VICTOR. The Highland warrior was the ideal man: fearless, faithful; and failed.

FLORA. If only your mother could see you got up so braw in her family tartan.

PEARL. He looks well in a skirt.

VICTOR. It is a kilt, Madam.

PEARL. You can romanticize failure all you like, Victor, but the fact is, we bear the mundane burden of success, with all its rights and responsibilities. If you're genuinely interested in your heritage, why not learn Gaelic? I'll tell you why not; because that would take work. The truth is, all the Highlanders with any get-up-and-go, got up and left years ago. They now run banks and shuffle documents. A waist-coated legion armed with briefcase and pince-nez.

VICTOR. *Poch ma hohn* [pron. pog ma hoyn] [trans: "kiss my arse."]

    FLORA *gasps.*

    Begging your pardon, Auntie. See, Pearl? I've been learning Gaelic.

FLORA. *Ainaibh ri cheile.* [pron. Eh-nev ree kaylee]

VICTOR. What does that mean?

PEARL. "I've been learning Gaelic."

VICTOR. Shutup. [*Nearly overlapping:*]

PEARL. Shutup.

VICTOR. Pearl –   PEARL. Pearl –

VICTOR. Act your age –   PEARL. Act your age –

VICTOR. Auntie – !   PEARL. Auntie – !

FLORA [*suprising fury*]. Eneuch!

> PEARL *and* VICTOR *stop, startled.* FLORA *is in deadly earnest.*

You've naebody but ilk ither noo. There's nane left but you twa. You maun look after one another. [*A beat. Cheerful once more:*] Victor, you must be faimished after your journey, and look at ya, ya wee skinnama-link, I'll go fix a plate –

PEARL. Auntie, don't bring the winkles in here, they're revolting.

FLORA. Winkles?

PEARL. Ay, winkles. You said Young Farleigh –

FLORA [*remembering her lie*]. Och ay, winkles! They were nane of 'em any good. Shells were empty.

PEARL. All of them?

FLORA. Pixies. Belike gobbled 'em up.

PEARL. "Pixies"? Why not fairies?

ACT I

FLORA. Fairies dinna eat winkles.

PEARL. Auntie, you find evolution far-fetched, yet you've no difficulty with your taxonomy of fairies, pixies and werewolves.

FLORA. There's no such thing as a werewolf.

VICTOR. No matter, Auntie, I've gone vegetarian.

PEARL [*muttering so Auntie won't hear*]. Got to be difficult, haven't you.

FLORA. Ma poor lad, shall I send for Dr Reid?

VICTOR. I'm fine, Auntie. I saw a play in London by an anti-vivisectionist; he annoyed so many people with his socialists, sensualists and suffragists that I wound up converted in spite of the fact he's an Irishman. So I'm no longer eating animals.

FLORA. I'll fetch a bit of cold mutton, then, shall I?

VICTOR. Any of your shortbread about?

FLORA. Fresh this morning! Now behave yourself, your sister's working.

> FLORA *exits.* VICTOR *takes a silver flask from his sporran and offers it to* PEARL. *She merely stares at him.*

VICTOR [*toasting her*]. "Scots wha' hae." [*drinks*]

PEARL. Don't let Auntie see that, it would kill her.

33

VICTOR. What's ailing her?

PEARL. She's cranky.

VICTOR. She's grieving, her brother died.

PEARL. Why ask, if you know? Auntie and I have been slaving here in a legal limbo with one foot in the poor house, waiting for you so Father's estate can be settled. Belle Moral doesn't run itself, you know. She's getting on.

VICTOR. Nay, she's spry; and she's got the full abacus upstairs, I can hear the beads rattling back and forth.

PEARL. Time does not stand still in your absence, Victor. You may manage to avoid growing up, but others do not. People age, fathers die.

A beat. He drinks.

VICTOR. What are you working on these days?

PEARL. I'm searching the coast for fossil evidence of transitional species.

VICTOR. Why not search the family plot?

PEARL. What have you done with yourself since the funeral? Apart from "roamin' in the gloamin'"?

VICTOR. I've been working.

ACT I

PEARL. Really and truly? Victor MacIsaac, if only Father could hear you say that. So you're finally taking your accountancy articles at MacVicar, MacVie, and MacVanish.

VICTOR. No. I'm writing.

PEARL. Writing what? A treatise?

VICTOR. A novel.

PEARL. In your spare time.

VICTOR. It takes up all my time.

PEARL. Father hated fiction.

VICTOR. I've dedicated it to Mother's memory.

PEARL. What's it about?

VICTOR. It's about an alienated young man who recognizes the meaninglessness of life.

PEARL. What's the plot?

VICTOR. The plot's not the point.

PEARL. You must have a plot or there's no point.

VICTOR. That's the point.

PEARL. Well something must happen.

VICTOR. He shoots a stranger on the beach for no reason.

PEARL. For no reason?

VICTOR. An Arab.

PEARL. Why an Arab?

VICTOR. Pure chance.

PEARL. That's absurd.

VICTOR. Precisely.

PEARL. Is he apprehended?

VICTOR. He wakes the next morning to find he's turned into a gigantic insect.

PEARL. Have you finished it?

VICTOR. I haven't started it.

PEARL. Well get on with it!

VICTOR. I can't. To write it would be an act of faith, thus undermining the integrity of the work.

PEARL. Yer a wastrel.

VICTOR. I'm the last honest man.

PEARL. A lazy loafer.

VICTOR. I am not.

PEARL. You've never finished a thing in your life.

VICTOR. Finishing is highly over-rated.

PEARL. You couldn't even finish with Father's death duties.

VICTOR. I'm here now, am I not?

PEARL. On your own sweet time.

ACT I

VICTOR. I almost didn't come back at all!

PEARL. You may fool yourself, Victor, but you don't fool me [*grabbing paper and pen from an escritoire, writing*]. I'll send for Mr Abbott. He'll bring Father's will tomorrow. No one will stand in your way again, you'll have no one to blame – you certainly won't have Father – [*sealing the note*] and we'll see what you accomplish with your new-found freedom.

VICTOR. Pearl –

PEARL [*yanking a bell cord, calling off*]. Young Farleigh!

VICTOR. Pearl! I really did want to stay away.

PEARL. Why?

VICTOR. Because... As long as I don't come home, I needn't feel... [*Tears threaten, he forces a smile.*] You see, Pearl, I only ever get homesick. When I come home.

PEARL. What's the matter, Victor? Don't you want Belle Moral?

VICTOR [*shaking his head*]. Yes [*nodding*]. And no. And yes. And no. And –

PEARL. Well which is it?

VICTOR. Both.

PEARL. You can't have both [*to off*]. Young Farleigh!

VICTOR. Why not?

PEARL. Because two opposite things cannot be true
at the same time.

VICTOR. Yes they can.

PEARL. They cannot.

VICTOR. Indeed they can.

PEARL. Canna.

VICTOR. Can.

PEARL. Then why did you come back?!

VICTOR. I had a dream.

PEARL [*exasperated*]. Oh, Victor.

VICTOR. I dreamt of Mother. At least, her voice
was there. What did she look like, Pearl?

PEARL. You know as well as I. She looked like that
[*the portrait*]. More or less.

VICTOR. No, Pearl. Tell it the right way.

PEARL ... [*starting to yield*]. She was beautiful. Like
a queen. That's why she was called Régine.

VICTOR. What did she sound like?

PEARL. She used to sing.

VICTOR. Sing the song, Pearl.

ACT I

PEARL. Not now, Victor.

Soft music: Au Claire de la Lune.

VICTOR. In my dream, I was wrapped up snug in
that old tartan shawl [*the painting*]. It was
warm like her voice. And soft, not rough as
you'd expect of a woolen blanket, but smooth
against my face. Like fur. I could smell it.
And I felt... [*overcome*] so well. And I woke
up thinking, Mother would have let me have
a puppy. [*weeping*] I know she would.

PEARL. Victor. Please don't cry, Victor, I'm sorry.
Damnit. [*singing*] "Au Claire de la lune, mon
ami, Pierrot. Prete moi ta plume, pour écrire
un mot. Ma chandelle est morte, je n'ai plus
de feu. Ouvre moi ta porte, pour l'amour de
Dieu."

> VICTOR *has been listening, rapt.* PEARL
> *makes a move: is she about to hug him?*
> *But* FLORA *enters with a tray of shortbreads*
> *and he transforms, ultra cheerful once*
> *more, leaving* PEARL *a little stung.*

FLORA. Here's a wee pick-an-dab, Victor, sweetie.

VICTOR [*suddenly macho*]. Ambrosia! [*Helping
himself.*] Pearl, take a proper photograph
of me and Auntie. [*Singing for* FLORA.]
"Green grow the rashes, O, The sweetest
hours that e'er I spend, Are spent amang
the lasses, O!"

FLORA, *giggling, delighted.*

PEARL [*renewed asperity*]. I've no time for high-land games, Victor, I've promised a cover photo for the next issue of "The Edinburgh Journal of Rules and Exceptions."

VICTOR [*genial*]. I hope you know you're drowning in a cultural backwater here.

PEARL. Dinna speak to me of cultural tarpits, ma kilted laddie.

VICTOR. I wear this relic in a spirit of pure irony, dear heart, as well as a sure-fire bid to irritate you to the depths of your Protestant soul.

PEARL. Edinburgh may not be at the centre of a great empire, but we are a modern city with a bittie of everything: art, science, golf. Not to mention a *leading* lunatic asylum; the patients perambulate freely about the grounds and in winter besport themselves on the curling rink. Nor have we any shortage of free-thinkers: there's an Italian [pron. Eye-talian] green grocer in Princes Street across from the Scott Monument, and you know Rhouridh [pron. Roo-oo-rrry] MacGregor, Jinnie MacGregor's cousin? He's become a nihilist. What a waste.

FLORA. That's what a papist comes to in the end.

ACT I

VICTOR. Father's dead, Pearl, you've no excuse now, get out and see the world, travel.

FLORA. She intends to book a camel.

PEARL. I can't go anywhere til you take responsibility for Belle Moral —

VICTOR [*enthusing*]. To hell with Belle Moral, Pearl the world is changing, it's cracking open, see it now so you'll know how unrecognizable it's about to become: the masses throbbing like a steam engine about to fly from the rails; men throwing off their shackles, women eschewing their corsets, clamouring for suffrage; humanity rising like sap or a lit fuse, and whether we burst into blossom or flame, who can tell? You sit here scribbling a note to send to town, meanwhile the products of the entire globe are at the fingertips of any toff in London with a telephone. Invention has outstripped its mother, necessity; the old ways and the old walls are tumbling, the lines are blurring; art and science set to flood their banks and mingle, can you imagine what their confluence might yield?

PEARL. Mud?

VICTOR. Look at Darwin. Thanks to him, science turns out to be stranger than a Greek myth: are we men or animals?

PEARL. Some of us are women, and we're all of us animals.

41

FLORA. We're not!

VICTOR. Science now tells us what art has been prophesying at the gates for years, namely that we can no longer take the evidence of our senses for granted.

PEARL. Science does that quite regularly. [*Enjoying the argument as much as he is.*] Until recently, mankind was flummoxed by the question: what is the basic substance of the universe? The apparent "Nothing" through which we and the planets move? The necessary "Something" which lends predictability to our mathematical calculations? *That* was the question.

FLORA. And, was there an answer?

PEARL. By dint of hard work, indeed there was.

VICTOR. What was it?

PEARL. Oh Victor, luminiferous ether, of course.

He's never heard of it, nor has FLORA.

VICTOR. Pearl, is it not just possible that this time art is leading the way?; hinting to us that your quest for "substance" might be entirely beside the point. Look at the impressionists–

PEARL. I'd rather not.

VICTOR. Then look at Mother's painting. Observe the brush strokes; each shimmering with possibility. Like a series of suggestions.

ACT I

Draw back and flux yields to stasis. A man, a woman, two children, solid and certain. Draw near and you lose the edges, so gradually do the colours blend one into another; as though they might give rise to any number of different pictures. Nearer still and they appear disconnected; a collection of random daubs, bald facts, meaningless. Until finally they are mere atoms that seem to dance before one's eyes. Light turns to matter, and matter to motion. Are we seeing the painting itself, or only one possibility of itself? Is the picture emerging? Or is it fading?

PEARL. I can't tell, it's too blurry.

VICTOR. So is life. Mother may have been years ahead of her time.

PEARL. She may have been short-sighted.

FLORA. Ay, she had a stigmata.

VICTOR. And what of the composition? Is it intentionally unbalanced as a comment on our family? Or did Mother mean to add another figure before she died?

FLORA [*slightly alarmed*]. What other figure? There is no other figure.

VICTOR. There's you, Auntie.

PEARL. It's clear enough to me: Mother never finished anything either.

VICTOR [*reasonable*]. You can't see Mother's painting because you're looking for vulgar like-
ness. As in your photograph.

PEARL. Don't compare Mother's painting with my
photograph. One is art, such as it is, the other is science.

VICTOR. Your photo isn't science, it's just bad art.

PEARL. In which case, Mother's painting is worse
science.

VICTOR. Not if science proves that reality is a blur
after all.

PEARL. Mother painted what she imagined. I photograph what is there. Art is subjective. Science is objective.

VICTOR. There's no such thing.

PEARL. Sir Isaac Newton and his apple; gravity;
the heliocentric movement of the planets;
heat expands, cold contracts, facts. Facts,
facts, facts. The scientific method yielding
real answers.

VICTOR. Who's asking the questions? What did
they have for breakfast?

FLORA. Kippers?

VICTOR. "To look at a thing is very different from
seeing a thing."

>   *A beat.*

ACT I

PEARL [*intrigued*]. Who said that?

VICTOR. Oscar Wilde.

PEARL [*dismissive*]. Another of your Irishmen.

VICTOR. There is nothing more contrived than realism.

PEARL. "Ism" be hanged, my photo is a true and perfect record.

VICTOR. Your photo may be a record. But Mother's painting is a map.

PEARL. Of what? The murky recesses of her psyche? What's the good of that?

VICTOR. Why does it have to be good for anything? Why can't it simply be beautiful and good for nothing? Like me.

PEARL [*returning to her camera, chipper*]. Stand up straight now, Victor, and try to look dignified, you're about to become extinct. Ah, I've got it. Get Mother's bagpipes down, Vickie, and make as though to woo Fate with the mournful tones.

VICTOR [*suddenly terribly offended*]. That's no' funny Pearl.

PEARL. What, I've always called you Vickie.

VICTOR. There's nothing humorous in Mother's bagpipes.

PEARL. Victor, I am not the mocker of the family. You are the one rendering risible one half your ancestry; I am attempting to immortalize it.

VICTOR [*verge of angry tears*]. Well you can't immortalize it, sister dear, because it's already dead.

He exits through the window.

FLORA. Now Pearl, you know he's sensitive about his mother.

PEARL. He never knew his mother, Flora.

FLORA. That's it, dear; she haunts him.

PEARL. I don't believe in ghosts.

FLORA. That's of nay concern to the ghosts.

VICTOR'*s kilt comes flying in through the window.*

FLORA. Poor Victor will catch his death of cold out there on the moor. [*Picking up the kilt.*] He's ne'er been strong i' the lungs.

PEARL. It's not his lungs that are exposed to the elements, Auntie.

An elderly man enters, slowly, carrying a silver tray with lid.

MAN [*to* PEARL]. You rang, Miss?

ACT I

FLORA. Young Farleigh; any sign of the good doctor?

YOUNG FARLEIGH. No' yit, M'um.

PEARL. Oh yes, the note. Take this to Mr Abbott in town as quickly as possible. [*a beat*] Perhaps I'll just run it in myself on my bicycle.

YOUNG FARLEIGH. Ay, Miss. [*Slowly goes to exit.*]

PEARL. Young Farleigh, who's the tray for?

> *He looks at the tray as though noticing it for the first time.* FLORA *comes to his rescue:*

FLORA. It's for Victor.

PEARL. Well don't waste your winkles, Victor's gone off them.

YOUNG FARLEIGH [*bewildered*]. Winkles? I've no' winkled in years, Miss.

FLORA [*pointedly*]. Nonsense, you were out half the nicht. [*to* PEARL] The Farleighs are all great winklers.

PEARL [*lifting the lid*]. Mmm, kippers and... boiled sweets. I'll have the fish in my study, you can give the gobstoppers to Victor.

YOUNG FARLEIGH. Is the lad come haim, then, Miss?

PEARL. I thought you said the tray was for –

FLORA. That will be all, Young Farleigh.

47

PEARL. Wait. I wish to consult you about a dog.

> FLORA *and* YOUNG FARLEIGH *exchange a look.*

I want you to find a puppy for my brother. A black one, about yea tall, with a flat head for patting.

YOUNG FARLEIGH. Ay, Miss.

> *Exit* YOUNG FARLEIGH. PEARL *lights a cigarette.*

FLORA. Must you, Pearl? It's so unladylike.

PEARL. Flora. [*Attempting a casual tone.*] Did Mother love me?

FLORA. Of course she did, sweetheart.

PEARL. She'd've loved Victor more.

FLORA. Your mother had love enough for a dozen bairns. But she'd scarce laid eyes on Victor's wee squallin' face 'afore she... was carried off.

PEARL [*critical*]. Mother was always weak.

FLORA. She was a great beauty. "Régine, Régine, my Highland Queen."

PEARL. I'll make it up to him with the puppy. Auntie, don't let Dr Reid leave without looking in, I've a question to put to him.

FLORA. Ay, pet.

PEARL [*pausing at the exit*]. Why have you sent for the doctor first thing in the morning? [*worried*] You're no' ill?

FLORA. Not at all. It's Young Farleigh. [*As though complicit.*] Ay, he's confused.

PEARL. Well, little wonder; it would appear that of late, no one gets a winkle of sleep under this roof. [*Exit.*]

> FLORA *takes* VICTOR's *flask from his sporran and has a sip. Regards the family portrait. Backs away from it. Examines it close up. Squints.* DR REID *exits, carrying his medical bag. They speak urgently, hurriedly.*

DR REID. Good morning –

FLORA. Dr Reid, oh thank God, thank you for –

DR REID. I came the moment I received your note, Flora, what is – ? [*hushed*] Where is Pearl?

FLORA. In her study.

DR REID. You've not told her.

FLORA. Certainly not.

DR REID. Flora, how in God's name – ?

FLORA. Twas my doing. I sent Young Farleigh to fetch her home.

DR REID. Why?

FLORA. I had no choice, Doctor; I couldna wrest another penny from the estate to pay for the poor creature's upkeep without first the will being settled, and there was no telling when Victor would –

DR REID. Why didn't you come to me?

FLORA. Ramsay would no' approve of charity –

DR REID. Charity?! I was his best –

FLORA. I know – I know – I know. [FLORA *begins to shiver.*]

DR REID. You need a cup of tea, or something stonger, [*calling*] Young Farleigh –

FLORA. Nay, let him be, he drove through the night. I'm well. Truly.

DR REID. Where have you put the... ? Where have you put her?

FLORA. In the attic.

DR REID. Under lock and key.

FLORA [*nods, "yes, pulling herself together*].

DR REID. Is it your intention, then, to house the... patient here, indefinitely?

FLORA. No, no, Victor's come haim this morning, so the will can be –

DR REID. Why then, 'twas all for naught.

ACT I

FLORA. Ach, you maun think me foolish. A foolish auld woman. Am I, Seamus?

DR REID. Foolish? In this case, Flora, perhaps yes. Old? [*kindly*] Never. For what would that make me, eh?

    A beat.

[*apprehensive*] How is she?

FLORA. She is... she's... I canna say, she's... quiet.

DR REID. Quiet.

FLORA. Ay. Wouldna' touch a bite o' breakfast.

DR REID. That's not surprising; the journey, the shock of new surroundings. Does she... has she spoken?

FLORA. Nay. Not a word.

DR REID. No cries, no... sounds, of any kind?

FLORA. Nothing.

DR REID ... How does she look?

    A beat.

Has there been any... change?

FLORA. Not apart from one might expect. Given the years. [*weeps*]

DR REID. Hush, Flora.

FLORA. I promised... Régine –

DR REID. We need not speak of it —

FLORA. I promised. To look after the children.

DR REID. And you have. Hush, now.

> YOUNG FARLEIGH *enters.*

YOUNG FARLEIGH. Mu'm, the doctor is [*sees* DR REID] here.

> *A woman screams in the distance.* FLORA *hurries toward the exit with* DR REID *in tow. But the cry is repeated and she rushes to the window.* YOUNG FARLEIGH *sinks onto a chair and closes his eyes.*

VOICES OFF. Help! Miss MacIsaac! Send for a doctor! A doctor!

FLORA. God help us.

DR REID [*joining her*]. What's happened? [*looking out*] Good Lord.

> *They exit.* YOUNG FARLEIGH *opens one eye. Lights change, he slowly rises and exits as* VICTOR *is carried on. Lights back up on:*

Scene 5 The Drawing Room

VICTOR *lies on the couch, naked and wet under a blanket.* DR REID *attends him.*

DR REID [*gently*]. Victor. Victor, lad, what is it, eh? A woman? Are you in debt lad, is that it? Or were you just pullin' a wee pliskie?

ACT I

VICTOR *covers his head with the blanket.*

DR REID. Come along now, son, the North Sea in April is hardly a congenial prospect, and I know you not to be a swimmer. What were you doing leaping from the rocks?

VICTOR [*soliloquizing from under the blanket*]. There are times when I cannot fathom why any sane person would choose to live out the natural length of their days. Life is an expanse of arid predictability, relieved now and again by hilarious and brutal jokes. This, we call tragedy.

DR REID. Go on.

VICTOR [*lowering the blanket, earnestly relishing his own words*]. I strayed along the barren beach and heard the kelpies singing, each... to each. And then they sang to me; a beckoning back to the dank, devouring womb of the sea; their sweet and deadly strains, the echo of my own futility. I parted the waters to mate with Nothingness.

DR REID. I see. How long have you felt this way?

VICTOR. I haven't been myself since the funeral.

DR REID. You miss your father.

VICTOR. I don't know if I'd go that far.

DR REID. How does the prospect of being master of Belle Moral cause you to... feel?

VICTOR. Like jumpin' into the sea.

DR REID. Victor, what would have become of your aunt and sister had you succeeded in your bid today? Who would look after them?

VICTOR. You would. They don't need me.

DR REID. Ah but they do. You'll find out soon enough, lad. Your father's burdens will soon be yours. But luckily, so will his oldest friend.

> VICTOR *takes his flask from under the quilt and drinks.* FLORA *enters with a bowl and spoon.* VICTOR *hides the flask.*

FLORA. How's ma poor laddie?

VICTOR [*feigning weakness*]. I feel I'm fading, Auntie.

FLORA. See if you canna tak a bittie o' parritch, ma hinnie.

VICTOR. I'll try.

DR REID. Have you no beef tea, Flora?

FLORA. Ay, but the lad's gone vegetative.

> PEARL *enters.*

PEARL [*brisk*]. He's fallen in with the Fabians. Armchair revolutionaries nibbling celery.

FLORA [*spoon poised*]. Here comes the coach-and-six, *clop-clop clop-clop...*

DR REID [*taking her aside*]. Pearl, I'm worried about your brother.

PEARL. As am I.

DR REID. Victor shows signs of neurasthenia: a degenerative instability which threatens the delicate edifice of brain and nerve.

PEARL. He gets that from Mother, no doubt.

> DR REID *does not immediately reply, reluct-ant to reveal to her the full extent of his concern.*

DR REID. He has confessed an attempted suicide.

PEARL [*loudly so* VICTOR *can hear*]. Dr Reid, my brother is suffering from nothing more than extreme foolishness and a common cold.

FLORA. Pearl, we're lucky your brother is alive. Ask Rhouridh MacGregor, who plucked him from the boiling sea.

PEARL. Saved by a nihilist. You ought to be ashamed.

DR REID. My dear Pearl, this is no way to treat a would-be suicide.

PEARL. Suicide, my eye. He ran down to the shore in high naked dudgeon for a little fleshly mortification, where he met Rhouridh Mac-Gregor out walking with his mother and his cousin, Jinnie. Victor leapt into the drink to hide from the ladies.

FLORA. Oh Victor.

DR REID. Is this true, sir?

VICTOR. Pearl, those are only the facts, and you know it!

DR REID. You've trifled with a man of science, Mr MacIsaac.

VICTOR [*indignant*]. The squalid circumstances of my brush with death merely confirm my despair at the human condition. Not for me a dignified death by drowning. Not for me to inspire the poet's lament, thus to snatch some meaning from the maw of death, no; I am the comic hero of a tragic farce. Plaything of a demented God who hasn't the decency to exist.

PEARL. Cheer up, Vickie; you've only your own carelessness to blame, not some cosmic vendetta.

DR REID [*picking up his bag*]. I'll take my leave now. My genuinely ill patients will be waiting.

VICTOR [*spritely*]. Still skookin' about the loony hoos, are you, Doctor?

PEARL. Victor.

VICTOR [*imitating her*]. "Edinburgh has a *leading* lunatic asylum."

DR REID. If you refer to the Royal Edinburgh Hospital, yes I am on staff as specialist in organic diseases of the mind.

VICTOR. What's that involve, then, amputatin' heads, are you? Is it true, Doctor, that a dog will lick the hand of the man who is vivisecting him?

DR REID. Good day.

> FLORA *is about to escort* DR REID *from the room.*

PEARL. Doctor, I've been puzzling over the ear you lent me.

> *A beat.* DR REID *and* FLORA *hesitate.*

Its length is out of proportion with its width at the base where it would attach to the skull. From this, I calculate a cranial circumferance commensurate with that of a microcephalous cretin. Does this strike you as reasonable?

DR REID [*momentarily at a loss*].

FLORA [*to the rescue*]. Dr Reid, you shouldna' go plyin' the lass with freaks of nature. It's no healthy for a young woman of child-bearing age.

PEARL. Really, Flora!

DR REID [*reassuring bedside manner*]. Now Flora, Pearl is gifted with the chief prerequisite of a scientific mind: curiosity. And what could be healthier, hm? Be sure to call me if you need anything –

PEARL. Doctor, I'm keen to compare this specimen with others of its kind –

DR REID [*too quickly*]. There are no others.

PEARL. Where did you obtain this one?

DR REID. ... From a friend.

PEARL. But where did the specimen originate?

DR REID. In a remote village. High in the Caucasus.

PEARL. I shall arrange an expedition; Father's bound to have left me an annuity –

DR REID. I know neither the name of the village, nor if it still –

PEARL. We'll ask your friend –

DR REID. He's dead.

PEARL. But he must have –

DR REID. Pearl, the ear is a mere curiosity. An accident of birth. It ought to excite more pity than wonderment.

ACT I

PEARL. Accidents are the very stuff of evolution. Darwin's work is far from done, Doctor, please. Help me.

DR REID. I'm afraid it's not in my line, Pearl. [*Almost to himself.*] Not anymore.

PEARL. Why hide your light under a bushel? Come with me to the Caucasus.

> *He gazes at her, but a dog barks, off, startling him and* FLORA.

You don't deserve a present, Victor, but you're my darling wee brother and I've got you one in spite of everything.

> YOUNG FARLEIGH *staggers on, hauling a long leash which thrashes about in his grasp. The barking is louder now.*

YOUNG FARLEIGH. Shall I bring him in, Miss?

PEARL [*unable to conceal her delight*]. I've got you a puppy, Victor.

VICTOR. A puppy! Oh Pearl, that's wonderful!

YOUNG FARLEIGH. Coal black, he is, with a head so flat, you could balance a teacup.

VICTOR. Here boy! Here – [*suddenly struggling for breath*].

> VICTOR *can't breathe.* DR REID *goes for his medical bag.*

DR REID. Take it away! Flora – !

FLORA [*rushing to assist* YOUNG FARLEIGH]. Out, out with it at once!

> *The leash snaps out of* YOUNG FARLEIGH*'s hand and whips off. He and* FLORA *hurry after it.* DR REID *injects* VICTOR *with a hypodermic needle.* VICTOR *goes* limp.

PEARL. My God, Doctor. If you hadn't been here...

> *He offers her a cigarette. She takes it, he lights it. They smoke and regain composure.*

DR REID. I've never seen such a severe phobic reaction.

PEARL. Phobic? But Doctor, a dog was Victor's one desire as a child, and it was his childhood's tragedy that Father refused him.

DR REID. Victor's desire for a canine companion was thwarted by your father; and, rather than admit defeat –

PEARL. Victor converted his desire into phobia.

DR REID. Just so, my dear; very good.

PEARL [*flattered*]. Thank you, Doctor.

DR REID. The thwarted little boy evolved into the phobic man. Your poor father.

PEARL. I should think Victor is in a better position to benefit from your sympathy.

ACT I

DR REID. Forgive me, I mean only to say that Victor is also in the sole position to inherit Belle Moral and pass on Judge MacIsaac's spotless name.

PEARL. Naturally Victor will inherit the MacIsaac estate, but I am just as capable of perpetuating the MacIsaac name.

DR REID. You've always been spirited, Pearl. Your father's one regret was that you were not born a son.

PEARL. I was as good as any son.

DR REID. Ay and better, more's the pity.

PEARL. Victor's not a bad fellow, he's just a little... artistic.

DR REID. I'm afraid it's worse than that. Victor may be an hysteric.

PEARL. But hysteria is a woman's disease.

DR REID. Right again, my dear, I've never heard of a case like his.

PEARL. That's our Victor for you. Always got to be an exception.

DR REID. If not an aberration. [*disturbed*] I wonder – is it possible – have I allowed the boy's natural high spirits – and my affection for him – to mask what ought to have been, to me as a physician, clear signs?

PEARL. What signs?

DR REID. The rapid oscillations betwixt melancholy and elation; his excessive sensuality; the obsession with his mother – not to mention the drink – and now this sudden aversion to animal food.

PEARL. Victor is merely panting after the latest avant-garde craze. He was quoting Oscar Wilde just now.

A beat. PEARL *misinterprets his silence:*

Flambouyant Irishman. Dramatist. Sports a velvet cape –

DR REID. Has Victor, to your knowledge, evinced a special fondness for any male companions?

PEARL. There's his old school chum, Rhouridh Mac-Gregor. But Victor has always been more at ease in the company of ladies.

A beat.

Rhouridh's not really a nihilist; just a sulky romantic. Decent chap. Carried a note into town for me just now.

A beat.

Dr Reid, Victor's passing fancy for Irishmen and and anti-vivisectionists –

DR REID. Anti-vivisectionists?

PEARL. He considers himself an ally of the under-dog.

DR REID. And an enemy of science. Not uncom-mon in the inebriate.

PEARL. This morning it was impressionists, yester-day it was mesmerists, and tomorrow it will be Egyptologists. Though it points to a fligh-ty nature, it hardly convicts him of hyste-ria.

DR REID. Admirably put. Might we not agree, how-ever, that your brother is of a highly strung temperament. [*tender*] So, too, was your mother. Promise me you'll keep a loving eye on him.

> FLORA *enters, winded.*

FLORA. We've caught the wee beastie and tied him in the paddock. [*sees* VICTOR] Victor!

DR REID. I've given him a mild sedative.

FLORA. Oh. Oh, thank God.

> YOUNG FARLEIGH *enters with a small silver tray. He takes a crumpled note from his pocket, places it on the tray, hands it to* PEARL.

PEARL. Excellent. Mr Abbott will come tomorrow and bring Father's will.

> FLORA *and* DR REID *exchange a look.* YOUNG FARLEIGH *sinks into a chair.*

DR REID. Pearl, I wonder if you oughtn't to put off the will for a few days. Until your brother's quite recovered.

PEARL. We could wind up putting it off indefinitely if your diagnosis is correct.

FLORA. What diagnosis?

PEARL. Victor is morbidly effeminate, Auntie, but that's not news. He requires a brisk dose of responsibility. Don't worry, Doctor, I'll make a man of Victor MacIsaac yet. One that's fit to inherit the stones of Belle Moral.

DR REID. Gently, Pearl.

PEARL. I think not. Fresh air, exercise and hard work.

DR REID. You gave me a bit of a turn just now.

PEARL. How so?

DR REID. For a moment you were your father. You were Ramsay all over.

PEARL. Thank you, Doctor.

> PEARL *exits, pleased with the compliment, but* DR REID *is slightly unsettled.*

FLORA. Seamus, what were you thinking, giving the lass that evil jar?

DR REID. You know what Pearl is like once her interest is piqued. What would you have had me do? Whisk it away with a portentous muttering?

FLORA. Why keep such a thing on your shelf in the first place?

DR REID. Perhaps as a reminder. Of what might have been... had I continued my work. [*Holding out his hand, summoning strength for what he is about to face.*] Come, Flora. Take me to her.

> FLORA *takes his hand just as* PEARL *enters to retrieve her camera. They part hands immediately.* PEARL *notices. They remain silent until she exits with her equipment.*

FLORA. Poor lassie. Her world will ne'er be the same after tomorrow.

DR REID. There is no good reason why Pearl should have to know the truth.

FLORA. Her brother's bound to tell her.

DR REID. Not if he's half the man his father was.

VICTOR [*sprawled, comatose*].

FLORA. Poor Victor's ne'er been able to keep a secret from anyone but himself.

DR REID. We must see that he does. We must also see that your unfortunate guest is returned to her rightful lodging as soon as possible. And Flora, get rid of that slavering cur.

They exit. PUPPY *barks in the distance. He stops,* VICTOR *wakes with a jolt. Recovers, only to be startled at the sight of* YOUNG FARLEIGH.

VICTOR. Young Farleigh. Young Farleigh.

He doesn't wake. VICTOR *tosses him the flask, he catches it.*

[*enjoying himself*] Go ahead. Go on. I'm to be master of Belle Moral and as such I order you to stop respecting me. Let's drink, comrade. Let us toast the inevitable decline of me and my bourgeois kind. Let us speak together as equals. And while you're at it, fetch me slippers.

YOUNG FARLEIGH [*toasting*]. *Aonaibh ri cheile.* [pron. ehnev ree kaylee] [*drinks*]

VICTOR. "*Aonaibh ri cheile*". What does that mean?

YOUNG FARLEIGH. Tis Gaelic.

VICTOR. I know "tis Gaelic", what in hell does it mean?

YOUNG FARLEIGH. Call yourself a Scot. [*another drink*]

VICTOR. When are we going to be rid of you? Snoolin' about the house, muttering Gaelic incantations, scorching the toast. And you're too decrepit to be out winkling in the night.

YOUNG FARLEIGH. Speak for yourself. [*another drink*]

VICTOR [*logical*]. I would but I haven't a clue who that is. There was a time, not so long ago, when man asked the question, "What is the meaning of life?" Now we ask, "Is there a meaning?" Look at me. I'm useless. But perhaps uselessness will turn out to have some evolutionary value. I can't know. Perhaps in a hundred years all the useful people will die of a plague that infects only those with a work ethic, and the useless will inherit the earth.

> *Pleased with himself,* VICTOR *reaches for the flask but* YOUNG FARLEIGH *keeps it and recites Robbie Burns with passion and surprising vigour.*

YOUNG FARLEIGH. "Wee, sleekit, cow'rin, tim'rous beastie,
O, what a panic's in thy breastie.
Thou need na start awa sae hasty,

Wi' bickering brattle.
I wad be laith to rin an' chase thee,
Wi' murd'ring pattle.

I'm truly sorry man's dominion
Has broken Nature's social union,
An' justifies that ill opinion
Which makes thee startle

At me, thy poor earth-born companion
An' fellow-mortal.

Pause.

But Mousie, thou art no thy lane,
In proving foresight may be vain;
The best laid schemes o' mice and' men
Gang aft a-gley.
An' lea'e us nought but grief an' pain
For promised joy.

Still thou art blest, compared wi' me.
The present only toucheth thee.
But och! I backward cast my e'e
On prospects drear.
An' forward, tho' I canna see,
I guess an' fear."

A beat. VICTOR *is awestruck.*

VICTOR. Are you my real father?

YOUNG FARLEIGH. Are you askin' me if you're a real bastard?

> *They laugh.* YOUNG FARLEIGH *gets up, crosses to* VICTOR, *hands him the flask, then punches him in the nose.* VICTOR *cries out in pain.*

That's for insulting your mother.

> *He goes to leave but* VICTOR *stops him, and speaks from the heart:*

VICTOR. Young Farleigh. Who was she? She was beautiful. She was a painter. That's all I have of her. I haven't even got the old shawl she wrapped me in.

>*A beat.*

YOUNG FARLEIGH. *Aonaibh ri cheile.* [pron. ehnev ree kaylee]

Scene 6 *The Attic Stairs*

A closed door at the top of a narrow staircase. The door opens. DR REID *emerges. He descends a few steps, then stops, sets down his medical bag and sits, devastated.* FLORA *emerges, pulls the door closed, then turns and sees* DR REID.

FLORA. Seamus... Come. I'll make you cup of –

DR REID. Flora.

>*A beat. She sits next to him, as he tries to collect his thoughts.*

This is her haim.

FLORA. Seamus. She canna byde here, not if –

DR REID. No, of course not, you're right, it's too too much to ask of you –

FLORA. 'Tisn't that. Ramsay said she was to be cared for – elsewhere – throughout the course of her natural life.

DR REID. To be sure, to be sure, but... what do we know of the place where she has been housed all these years?

FLORA. It's... decent.

DR REID. But you've ne'er seen it, ne'er –

FLORA. Young Farleigh –

DR REID. And he is the only one who ever visited.

> FLORA, *ashamed.*

Now, now, that was Ramsay's decision.

FLORA. But I didna wish to visit, Seamus. I kept awa'. I promised Régine I would look after the children. But the truth is, all these years, I've wished her dead. And God forgive me, I wish it still [*weeping*].

DR REID. You're only human, Flora, you did your best. [*regretful*] And so did I. But we've a chance now to do a bit better, eh? [*a beat*] Flora, what if she were to come live with me? As my patient? She would have the best of care. My laboratory overlooks the sea. You could visit, or not, as you pleased. And you could rest easy in your mind.

> *A beat.*

FLORA. Victor would have to agree.

DR REID. That's certain. I may need your help on that front. The lad has conceived a mistrust of me as a physician – not surprising, given his mental... [*delicate for* FLORA*'s sake*] fragility.

FLORA. Fragility? Surely he's more headstrong than fragile.

DR REID. I'd have said so myself before the events of this morning. [*urgent*] Flora, he is so like his mother. Sensitive, passionate...

FLORA. Niver say it, Seamus.

DR REID. I dread the morrow. For the lad will be master here and, as such, he'll have to be told.

FLORA. I dinna relish the telling.

DR REID. Nor do I, lest the shock precipitate another fit.

FLORA. Why must he be told at all? Ach, I ought ne'er to've brought the poor creature haim–

DR REID. Nay, Flora, you did the right thing. The humane thing.

FLORA. I ought to've turned to you sooner, Seamus, I know it, but I beg of you now, dinna desert us in our hour of need.

DR REID. I'll never desert this family, Flora.

Scene 7 Pearl's Study

Night. PEARL *is at her desk with the jar and a pile of open books.* PUPPY*'s nose jostles her elbow from behind the desk.*

PEARL. Lie down. Down.

> PUPPY *jostles her once more.*

> [*matter-of-fact*] I'll have to get Young Farleigh to drown you, I suppose.

> PUPPY*'s tail wags from behind the desk. She pats him on the head.*

There. [*business-like*] Now bugger off.

> *A knock at the door.*

What?!

> *The door opens,* FLORA *puts her head in.*

FLORA. Do go to bed, pet.

PEARL. I can't, Auntie, I'm working.

FLORA [*sees the dog*]. There it is, oh thank goodness. Here, come now, come. Come.

PEARL. He won't come, he's stupid as a post.

FLORA. Well he canna stay, not with Victor's phobia.

PEARL. I'll not allow him near Victor, Auntie.

FLORA. You're no thinkin' to keep him?

PEARL. Certainly not. [*Concealing her eagerness.*] Just overnight.

FLORA. I dare say Dr Reid would disapprove.

PEARL. What were you two whispering about so passionately this morning?

> FLORA *doesn't answer.*

> Nevermind, Auntie, I know and I don't mind a bit.

FLORA. You don't? You do? What don't you know?

PEARL [*teasing, affectionate*]. He's courting you. Holding hands, and who knows what jouker-ie-pawkerie –

FLORA. Pearl –

PEARL. And you needn't be jealous of the ear. It was a purely platonic gift.

> PUPPY *sniffs the jar,* PEARL *taps his nose.*

FLORA. Ach, Dr Reid never – he was merely – he was comehitherating with me over some woman's trouble.

PEARL. What woman?

FLORA. Why, me.

PEARL. Auntie, you've no taken ill. You have. [*stricken*] Oh, Auntie –

FLORA. Now, pet I've no' took ill, it's just... the change.

PEARL. Oh.

FLORA. Ay. [*Mopping her brow.*] No need to worry your head, that's a long way off for you.

PEARL. Any of your shortbread about, Auntie?

FLORA. Victor ate it up.

PEARL. Damn him.

> PUPPY *knocks over the jar with his paw.*

> Off, I said. [*On second thought:*] Here. [*Holding the jar out to him.*] What do you make of that?

FLORA. Pearl! [*covering*] It's bedtime. You don't want to be baggy-eyed and forfochen when Mr Abbott arrives first thing in the morning.

PEARL. What on earth does it matter? Although you'd do well to get your beauty rest, Auntie, if Doctor Reid is to join us.

FLORA. Hush your haiverin', noo. [*embarassed, pleased*] Pearl. You dinna truly reckon Dr Reid... harbours a speecial regard for your auld auntie?

PEARL. In my scientific opinion, it could not be more obvious.

BELLE MORAL

sh me to suppress the late Judge
s will?

ly not. I ask only that you delay
g long enough for the course of
ness to become apparent. If his
deteriorate, he can be delivered
care before ever tasting the bit-
inheritance. Your father would
were he here.

my father, Doctor.

s family has suffered enough.
humane sin of ommission and
a world of pain: misplace the
weeks.

suggest is not merely impossi-
usible; no one for a moment
me capable of misplacing any-

hattels await the heir to Belle
ht prove too much for the lad.

els"?

ings.

?

78

FLORA. Go on with you.

PEARL. Goodnight, Auntie.

FLORA. Goodnight, pet. [*Exit.*]

PEARL. Puppy, did you know that the name of Dr Darwin's ship was The Beagle? Darwin sought to penetrate that "mystery of mysteries", the appearance of new species. He proved that all life transforms by slow degrees into all other life. You came from the wolf. I came from the ape. But if the dinosaurs hadn't mysteriously vanished, we mammals might have remained a race of rodents. And in the absence of man, might the dinosaurs have developed higher consciousness? Perhaps certain traits are like secrets that will out, ideas that are bound to surface. If Darwin hadn't gone to the Galapagos, he'd have been a scientific footnote; if Shakespeare hadn't been caught poaching, he'd have been a wool merchant. But I'll wager there'd still be a father of evolution – or even a mother – and someone whom we call the Bard. Behave, now, or it's into the cellar with you. Lots of people thought of evolution before Darwin took all the seemingly unrelated bits and put them together in just the right way, at just the right time. His own grandfather, Erasmus Darwin, believed in the mutability of species. But his reasoning was flawed: he put a piece of vermicelli in a jar and waited to see if it would come to life. No one could take him seriously after that. [*chuckle*] Vermicelli. Dr Reid might have feared the same fate when he put his jar aside forever. [*About to place the jar back on the desk, a thought occurs to her.*] Puppy... have you ever seen an ape with the ear of a wolf? Nor have I...

Scene 8 The Drawing Room

The next morning. MR ABBOTT *is waiting. He is fastidiously groomed, wears a pince nez, and carries a leather briefcase.* DR REID *enters.*

DR REID. Ah, Mr Abbott, a word sir –

ABBOTT. Good morning, Doctor –

REID. It appears you failed to receive the note I sent you, last –

ABBOTT. I received it.

DR REID. Why, then, your reply must have gone astray.

ABBOTT. No, my reply is forthcoming, to wit: it is more than a little irregular to seek to embargo a will before the contents are known.

DR REID. But you know the contents –

ABBOTT. I do not, Doctor. My late father drew up Judge MacIsaac's will –

DR REID. Forgive me, I ought to have –

76

ABBOTT. Rumours. To do with the late Mrs Mac-Isaac. They do not bear repeating.

DR REID. Then a gentleman need not so much as allude to them, sir.

ABBOTT. A gentleman would not have me compromise my professional integrity, sir.

DR REID. I am a doctor. I too have integrity to uphold, indeed an oath: "First, do no harm." I beg of you, heed it.

FLORA *and* PEARL *enter.*

PEARL. Mr Abbott, good morning to you, sir.

ABBOTT [*bowing*]. Miss MacIsaac. [*and to* FLORA] Miss MacIsaac.

FLORA. Will you take a drop of coffee, Mr Abbott? [*Yanking the cord, hollering.*] Young Farleigh! Refreshments in the drawing room!

ABBOTT [*to* PEARL]. Miss MacIsaac, may I venture to express how immensely diverting I found to be your lecture on "Cambrian Invertebrates: A Comparative Anatomy of Stomachs and Guts".

PEARL. Why thank you, Mr Abbott.

ABBOTT. Incidentally, have you read Mr Edgar Allen Poe's, "The Conchologist's First Book: —"?

PEARL. "A System of Testaceous Malacology", I couldn't put it down.

ABBOTT. Nor could I.

PEARL. Mr Abbott, I had no idea you were a fossil enthusiast.

ABBOTT [*blushing*]. Indeed, I've conceived a passion for... paleontology.

DR REID. Where's Victor?

FLORA. I let him sleep late. The laddie's still on the delicate side.

VICTOR [*singing lustily from off*]. "Oh you tak the high road and I'll tak the low road and I'll be in Hades afore ye!"

> VICTOR *enters, bare-chested, kilted, wearing a tartan sash as a turban, the bridge of his nose bandaged where* YOUNG FARLEIGH *punched him.*

PEARL. Victor, you're drunk.

VICTOR. Oddly, no. I am about to become the Sultan of Belle Moral. Today I inherit Daddy's noble pile, so let a thousand and one Scottish nights begin. Every true Scot knows the bagpipes originated in Arabia.

FLORA. They never did.

VICTOR. Abbott, [*clapping his hands twice*] on with the show. Reveal the will of our father.

ACT I

DR REID clears his throat. ABBOTT ignores him, pulls a document from his briefcase, adjusts his pince nez, and reads:

ABBOTT. "Whereas I, Ramsay MacIsaac – "

VICTOR. Don't worry, Pearl, I'll no turn you oot o' hoos and haim.

ABBOTT. " – being of sound mind – "

VICTOR. I intend to throw wide the doors and let the twentieth century blow hard through the halls.

PEARL. Hush, Victor.

ABBOTT. " – do hereby designate the disposal of my worldly goods – "

VICTOR. I shall put an ad in The Times: "All Welcome".

ABBOTT. " – my will to be executed by Mr Edward Abbott, senior solicitor of Abbott, Abbott, Brodie and Bloom, except that, in the event that he predecease me, my will to be executed by his son, Mr Lorenzo Abbott."

VICTOR and PEARL exchange a look, stifle a giggle, "Lorenzo"?

"I was born heir to solid Protestant traditions, the transmission of which from father to son ensured my portion in this world and the next. But in a moment of weakness I cast my seed upon stony ground. I broke the

81

pure chain of descent and sullied the Mac-
Isaac bloodline in an unholy alliance with
the papist, Régine MacPhail. For my wayward desire have I atoned enough in life – "

VICTOR. God bless wayward desire!

ABBOTT. " – but that atonement must extend beyond the grave. My one break with holy tradi-
tion can be set right by one more such break:
to this end do I disinherit my son, Victor
MacIsaac. Upon my daughter Pearl whose
parts recommend her as a true MacIsaac,
do I bestow Belle Moral and all its goods
and chattels. With one condition: that the
sins of the mother not be visited upon the
daughter, it is my will that she remain child-
less. In the event that she bear progeny, my
estate to revert to the Presbyterian Kirk."

Shock. VICTOR *exits through the window.
A beat, then* FLORA *follows.*

Miss MacIsaac... good day. [*aside to* DR REID]
As you can see, Doctor, you underestimated
Ramsay MacIsaac. He was every bit as hu-
mane as you.

ABBOTT *exits.*

DR REID. Pearl –

PEARL [*crisp, as though nothing had happened*].
Doctor Reid, I've had an insight into the ear–

ACT I

DR REID. It's a tragedy you'll never be a mother. 'Tis every woman's dearest wish –

PEARL. It has never been mine. You insist the ear is a mere curiosity, but –

DR REID. Pearl –

PEARL [*acid*]. Well what would you have me do, Doctor? Weep and moan 'cause I'll never be saddled with a welter of brats mewling for "Mummy"? I only wish Father, in his munificence, hadn't entirely disinherited Victor; it'll feed the boy's romantic martyrdom and give him an excuse to drink himself to death at my expense. I suppose that's why Father cut me off at the ovaries: to prevent me spawning a breed of hysterical little boys. [*suddenly struck*] Doctor...

DR REID. What is it?

PEARL. Was there – ? There was madness in Mother's family, wasn't there?

DR REID. Your mother was a beautiful woman.

PEARL. Ay, beautiful and mad. Victor is the picture of Mother; you think he's mad.

DR REID. Unstable, perhaps.

PEARL. Doctor. [*apprehensive*] Will I go mad?

DR REID. No, no, my dear, you're the picture of Ramsay.

PEARL. How did she die?

DR REID. You know quite well, she –

PEARL. She contracted child-bed fever when Victor was born.

DR REID. Ay, that's what carried her off.

PEARL. You needn't euphemize on my account, Doctor. How soon after onset does death normally occur?

DR REID. A matter of hours, Pearl, she didn't suffer long.

PEARL. Yet I'm to believe Mother had time and strength to paint Victor into the family portrait before being "carried off"? I'll warrant she was carried off, the question is "to where?" The Royal Edinburgh Asylum. Tell me, Doctor. Is she alive? And put away?

DR REID. No she is not, you have my word. As to the portrait; Régine painted the infant into it before she gave birth. After all, she knew she was with child.

A beat.

PEARL. If not mad then what was she? Immoral?

DR REID. No –

PEARL. "The sins of the Mother", she had to've been either fallen or mad, which was it?

DR REID. Neither.

PEARL [*angry*]. Then what did Father mean?!

DR REID. He merely wished to protect you.

PEARL. From what?!

DR REID. The laws of heredity are such that... a flaw may lurk undetected for generations.

PEARL. You mean I could breed a crop of lunatics.

DR REID. You said yourself you'd no desire for bairns.

PEARL [*mounting fear*]. It's in me too, isn't it?

DR REID. Pearl –

PEARL. The flaw.

DR REID. Hush –

PEARL. "Lurking."

DR REID. Pearl. You know I've been fond of you since you were a girl. I was your father's dearest friend; I know he'd give his blessing.

PEARL. To what?

DR REID. I want to marry you, Pearl.

PEARL [*nonplussed*]... Why?

DR REID. Oh Pearl, there's so much to live for, so much of beauty and wonder. I want to share it with you.

PEARL. What have we to share?

DR REID. Our work. [*passionate*] You were right. I have been hiding. My dearest girl, I hope you may never have cause to learn how the sweetness can drain from the cup of life so gradually as to go unnoticed. Until one day that cup is empty. But now... Oh my dear, a great journey awaits us.

PEARL. To... the Caucasus?

DR REID. The journey between one cell and another can far outdistance that between the poles of the earth. Pearl, I shall lay my entire laboratory at your feet. I'll instruct you in the art of dissection. We'll establish our own institute of scientific inquiry, here at Belle Moral; bypass the graybeards in London who are too antiquated in their views to recognize that, in matters of intellect, woman is the equal of man. We'll toil side by side and I will cherish you as the alchemist of old cherished his *soror mystica*, my mystical sister. My equal.

PEARL. But Doctor —

DR REID. Seamus.

ACT I

PEARL. We can do all of that without benefit of clergy, without... [*an awkward beat*]

DR REID. I would not touch a hair of your head, my dear. My passion is not of the flesh, but the mind.

> *A beautiful young man enters, dressed exactly as* YOUNG FARLEIGH *was, carrying a covered tray.*

YOUNG MAN [*solemn*]. Refreshments.

PEARL. Who the devil are you?

YOUNG MAN. Young Farleigh's grandson, Miss. Wee Farleigh.

ACT II

Scene 1 Pearl's Study

That night. Moonlight. The door swings open. A FIGURE *enters, crouched, a worn tartan shawl draped about its head and shoulders. Audible breathing – almost a panting – as though an effort were being made to control fear and maintain silence. Sniff-sniff. Silence. The* FIGURE *explores the room, dropping to crawl on all fours, pausing here and there. It arrives at* PEARL*'s desk and is stopped by the sight of the jar. Reaches for it. Fumbles with it.* FLORA *appears in the doorway with an oil lamp. The* FIGURE *looks up and drops the jar.*

FLORA. There you are. Thank God. [*Firm but gentle.*] Come, now. Come.

> *The* FIGURE *rises and starts toward* FLORA*'s outstretched hand.*

Here now. Give them to me.

> *The* FIGURE *reaches out and hands* FLORA *her ring of keys.*

Scene 2 *Pearl's Study*

Next morning. PEARL *enters and spots something on the floor. She takes tweezers from her desk, bends and carefully picks up the ear.*

PEARL [*bellowing to off*]. Wee Farleigh!

> WEE FARLEIGH *enters with a frilly tray.*

Where is that slavering cur?

WEE FARLEIGH. Out frolicking, Miss.

PEARL. Well find it and beat it. No. Put it in a sack and drown it. What's that?

WEE FARLEIGH [*formal, well-mannered, yet somehow seductive*]. Breakfast, Miss. Earl Gray tea. Coddled eggs. Brioche –

PEARL. What?

WEE FARLEIGH. A bun. Only better.

PEARL. Oh. [*a beat*] Well, take it away, I'm... [*wave of nausea*].

WEE FARLEIGH. Feeling poorly, Miss?

PEARL. Do as I say.

> *He goes to exit with the tray.* PEARL *catches sight of something else, bends and retrieves the lid and the empty jar, perfectly intact.*

Wee Farleigh. You needn't drown it, just... give him away to anyone who wants him.

WEE FARLEIGH. Ay, Miss.

Scene 3 Hallway / The Attic Stairs

FLORA *and* DR REID *enter, heading for the attic stairs.* WEE FARLEIGH *enters with a pot of coffee.* FLORA *and* DR REID *step back out of sight, allowing* WEE FARLEIGH *to cross before they mount the stairs, resuming their conversation:*

FLORA. I was wushin' the poor creature in the tub–

DR REID. The tub?

FLORA. In the old nursery – not to worry, it's quite out of the way – I'd doffed ma dress, if ye maun know, down to ma linens so's not to drench mis-sel, and scarce had I turned my back when she lifted ma keys. [*A touch of admiration.*] For a' that she's meek, she's clever.

DR REID [*admonishing*]. She's cunning. What if she'd – ?

FLORA. There was no harm done.

DR REID. Next time get Wee Farleigh to help you with the bathing.

FLORA. Wee Farleigh? That's hardly decent.

DR REID. And in future, confine her ablutions to the attic. Use a basin. Do not lavish upon her, luxuries to which she is insensible.

FLORA. Ach, I was anerly tryin to make the poor lamb presentable.

DR REID. For whom?

FLORA. Why, for Pearl.

A beat.

It's this morning I'll be telling her. You'll help me, won't you, Seamus? I fear to tell her on my own.

DR REID. Need you tell her at all?

FLORA. She'll have to know now she's mistress here.

DR REID. Not necessarily. Not if I am master.

A beat as FLORA *takes in the implications.*

FLORA. Ach Seamus, you're old enough to be the lassie's faither.

DR REID. And that is what I shall be to her. A second father. I shall guide her studies and stimulate her mind to fructify as her womb never shall.

FLORA. Ay, but... [*resisting tears*] I always pictured a bonnie lad. One who'd awaken her heart and bring a flush to her cheek, a sigh to her lips –

DR REID. She's thirty-two years old, Flora. Barren and waist-deep in the sands of time.

ACT II

> VICTOR *enters in his bathrobe, badly hung-over, the bridge of his nose bandaged, nursing a cup of coffee. He is stopped by their voices behind the door to the attic stairs, and listens.*

FLORA. Ay, so she's old enough to hear the truth.

DR REID. She's a woman for a' that.

FLORA. As am I, and have I not borne the horror of it?

DR REID. Ay but the horror does not lurk within your very loins.

FLORA [*stung*]. How would you know the first thing about my loins? Mayhap the flaw did come from my brother's side, he was the one with the Faery hair!

> *A beat.* DR REID *gives her a look at once indulgent and reproachful.*

Has she given you an answer?

DR REID. Not yet. For heaven's sake, Flora, I am proposing to lift the burden from your shoulders, to shield this family from calumny and pain, is not that your dearest wish and mine?

FLORA. Ay...

> DR REID *mounts the stairs, turns and waits for her to follow.* VICTOR *exits.*

Scene 4 *Pearl's Study*

PEARL *is seated, leaning forward, head between her knees.* VICTOR *rushes on.*

VICTOR. Pearl, I must have a talk with you – ! What's the matter?

PEARL [*sitting up*]. You look like a dog's breakfast.

VICTOR. You're white as a sheet.

PEARL. I am blanched with disappointment, but quite prepared to hear your apology.

VICTOR. For what?

PEARL. You know perfectly well for what, you and your petty revenge, I had nothing to do with Father's will, Victor, it came as just as much of a shock to me as it did to you.

VICTOR. I don't care about the damn will.

PEARL. Well you ought to. [*Pointedly returning to her work.*] Don't worry, I'll have Abbott arrange a suitable annuity for you.

VICTOR. Fine. Pearl –

PEARL. You'll not have a penny for liquor though, my boy.

VICTOR. I'll drink myself to death if I damn well please.

PEARL. Not on my money, you won't.

VICTOR. I don't want your stinkin' money.

PEARL. No brother of mine will traipse about like a bohemian; I'll no' give you the satisfaction of being poor.

VICTOR. Do shutup –

PEARL. And I'll thank you not to go rummaging among my specimens.

VICTOR. I wouldn't touch your gruesome specimens with a ten-foot pole.

PEARL. You were in fooling with the ear last night.

VICTOR. I was not – What "ear"?

PEARL. This ear, here! You're lucky it didn't turn to jelly overnight.

VICTOR. I never touched it.

PEARL. You did.

VICTOR. I didna.

PEARL. Did so.

VICTOR. Did –

PEARL. How many opposable digits are there in this household?!

VICTOR. What?

PEARL. Thumbs! Mankind's distinguishing tool; thumbs! wrought by aeons of natural selection; thumbs! to raise us up above the beasts.

And you can find no better use for yours than to steal about in the night twistin' the lids offa jars. [*Cutting him off.*] You did so! And Puppy took the blame. Poor Puppy.

VICTOR. Where is he?

PEARL. Don't worry, Victor, Wee Farleigh's got him on a leash. At the bottom of the pond.

> VICTOR, *shocked.*

You're too suggestible, Vickie.

VICTOR. I hope it does come out in you.

PEARL. What?

VICTOR. The "flaw", the family curse.

PEARL. What do you know about it?

VICTOR. I heard Dr Reid talking to Auntie Flora. She wants to tell you the truth about our family, and he won't let her. He's up to something.

PEARL. I know the truth.

VICTOR. You do? What is it?

PEARL [*dismissive*]. I can't tell you, you couldn't take the shock.

VICTOR. I could too, I'm as much a man as you. Pearl, I've a right to know.

PEARL. It's for your own good, Victor.

Victor. Tell me.

PEARL. No.

VICTOR. Tell me.

PEARL. Nay.

VICTOR. I'll make you – [*grabbing the jar*].

PEARL. Give it – !

> *He begins to have difficulty breathing, eyes fixed on the jar.*

[*disgusted*] Hypochondria: the last refuge of the scoundrel.

> *He is gasping.*

Victor, control yourself or you really will have a –

> *He is asphixiating.*

Auntie! Wee Farleigh! Someone!

> *She tries to wrest the jar from his grasp.*

Scene 5 The Drawing Room

FLORA, PEARL, *and* WEE FARLEIGH *are gathered round* VICTOR *who goes limp on the couch.* DR REID *withdraws the needle from* VICTOR'*s arm and returns it to his medical bag.*

DR REID. These fits are a terrible strain on the heart.

FLORA. Pearl, why did you let your brother look at the ear?

PEARL. I didn't "let" him do anything, Auntie, he's a grown man. What are we to do, Doctor, he can't go on like this, what's to become of him out in the world, hysterical and swallowing his tongue every five minutes, is there no cure?

DR REID. For hysteria in the male? Not yet.

PEARL. If he were a woman you could snip out his uterus and be done with it.

DR REID. There are specialists in Europe.

PEARL. Where?

DR REID. At the Sal Petrière in Paris. They've had promising results with the galvanic battery, but –

FLORA. We'll no' send your brother to be keyed awa' in a fremmit loony hoos!

DR REID. Dear Flora, there is no reason why you should be capable of imagining the fear, the keening sorrow, the harm that awaits a patient like Victor should his illness go untreated. But I have seen it, and all too often.

PEARL. Doctor, I would accompany my brother to the antipodes and back if I thought it would cure him, but I cannot pin my hopes on an

asylum, whether here or on the continent –
Victor would become completely hysterical
if we sought to admit him for so much as a
consultation.

DR REID. Mm. Puts me in mind of an old case history I came across recently. A patient faced
the prospect of living out her days in a cheerless institution, or dwelling amid her family who were quite ill-equipped to provide
for her... unusual medical needs. So the physician in the case offered to take the patient
in and care for her in his own home.

PEARL. Doctor, such an offer – if that is what you
intend – surpasses generosity, but I cannot
see Victor consenting to such an arrangement.

DR REID. Nor, frankly, can I.

FLORA [*apprehensive*]. And did he?

DR REID. What's that, Flora?

FLORA. Did the Doctor take her in?

DR REID. Oh, as it happened, he was called away,
and the family was left to bear their burden
alone. It ended badly, I'm afraid.

PEARL. Don't worry, Auntie, I'll not send Victor
away, nor will he languish here. If we cannot go to the asylum, let the asylum come to
us. We'll import the finest therapies, regardless of expense, and rearrange Belle Moral

to suit his needs. I'll make an artist's studio for him in the attic, see to it he doesn't indulge excessively in spirits, we'll purge the estate of dogs, and Dr Reid will direct his care, won't you, Doctor?

DR REID. Of course. I'll make regular house calls. In between my other commitments. And providing I am not called away to the continent.

PEARL. You see, Auntie? Everything will be all right.

FLORA. Pearl, we canna care for your brother here on our own.

PEARL. For pity's sake, Flora, make up your mind.

FLORA. There's more to... there are things beyond your ken, pet.

PEARL. What "things"?

A beat.

FLORA. Have you considered Dr Reid's proposal?

PEARL *at a loss, looks from* FLORA *to* DR REID.

DR REID. I spoke to your aunt, Pearl. I did think it proper.

PEARL. Of course. [*to* FLORA] Dear Auntie, I...

DR REID [*to* WEE FARLEIGH]. I think we could all do with a cup of tea.

ACT II

PEARL. Auntie, I know you cherish certain other... hopes. And, though I'd thought to speak first to Dr Reid in private, I wish you both to know that I –

FLORA. Marry him, Pearl.

PEARL. What?

FLORA. Dr Reid will live here and look after Victor, he'll look after... everything.

PEARL. Wh – why? You think me incapable?

FLORA. No, no –

PEARL. Sheltered and ignorant because I've dedicated my life to study rather than gad about the world like Victor – much good it's done him. I'll have you know there is a greater distance between two cells than between the poles of the earth –

FLORA. Pearl –

PEARL. I am mistress of Belle Moral! My father *willed* me capable. You would have me forego my inheritance, my chance to consecrate myself to my work – forgive me, Doctor, your proposal does me nothing but honour, I speak on principle only –

FLORA. Pearl, there's more to life than work.

PEARL. You'd rather I were more like your precious Victor; sensual, dissolute –

FLORA. Nay, pet –

PEARL. Dismissing my work as if it were just another lady-like "accomplishment" on a par with playing the pianoforte, "mind you don't get *too* accomplished, dear, and frighten the young gentlemen away –

DR REID. Pearl, I'm eager to hear of your insights into the ear.

FLORA. Don't encourage the lass.

PEARL [*to* FLORA]. If you can't stomach science, go back to your elves and pixies and – !

DR REID. Now, Pearl, don't be too hard on your auntie, she is of another generation.

FLORA [*to* DR REID]. So are you.

PEARL [*almost feverish with excitement*]. Doctor, I have indeed been vouchsafed a fresh insight into the ear which I am longing to share with you.

DR REID. I am longing to receive it.

PEARL. You claim it is more than a freak, meaningless –

DR REID. Not meaningless, no. Indeed, no, no, no, it is pregnant with meaning.

PEARL. What kind of meaning?

DR REID. Pearl. Even now there are those among us whose bodies function as evolutionary Trojan Horses, concealing traits that harken back to a common ancestor. Not only of man. But of every mammal on Earth.

PEARL. You think the ear is a throwback?

DR REID. I think it likely.

PEARL. Victor's fit proves the ear is canine –

DR REID. Victor's fit proves that he *perceived* the ear to be canine. As such it may say more about him than about the ear. Indeed, is the fit merely one side of the phobic coin? Heads: an unwholesome fear of canines in particular. Tails: an unwholesome identification with animals in general, witness his new-found vegetarianism.

PEARL. We're all of us animals.

DR REID. Touché, my dear; we differ in degree only, not in kind. But if Man does not cast off the vestiges of his animal origins, he can only revert; back to the beast.

PEARL. But how do we know which vestiges to cast off? We are all changing – evolving – even now, in this drawing room. Life teems at the uncertain line between species, and who's to say it's a line at all, perhaps it's more of a... blur. The bones of my hand with which I take up a pen or wield a paint brush are the same that propel a bat to fly, a horse to gallop, a whale to swim. Darwin said "we shall never probably disentangle the inextricable web of affinities between the members of any one class."

DR REID. That doesn't mean we should not try.

PEARL. Of course not, but what is it we are supposed to glean from these endless variations? – [*wonderment*] apart from an odd disequilibriating sense of déja vue; such as when we gaze upon the countenance of a great ape.

A beat.

FLORA [*likewise in wonderment*]. I've seen the photo of those monkeys drinking tea in the London Zoo. All got up in top hats and bonnets. I've never been so disequi-liberated.

PEARL. Perhaps Victor's phobia is an effect of his overheated mythopoetical faculty; it having rendered him susceptible to a deep recognition of animal kinship.

A beat.

DR REID. Intriguing.

PEARL. Canines, of course, are invested with supernatural significance in many cultures including our own, frequently as psychopomps.

ACT II

FLORA. Who?

DR REID. Guides between this world and the next.

PEARL. Guardians at the gates of the Underworld. Witness the Greeks with their three-headed dog, Cerberus, who was soothed by music; the Egyptians with Anubis, an imposing creature with the head of a Jackal and the body of a man. Often depicted carrying baked goods.

FLORA. Baked goods?

> WEE FARLEIGH *enters, carrying tray with tea, and piled high with pastries.*

WEE FARLEIGH. Baked goods.

PEARL. For the journey into the afterlife. What is the secret these mythic creatures keep? [*Takes a pastry.*]

FLORA. Who? The apes or the pompadours?

PEARL. And how are we to winkle it out of them? What is the – [*taking a bite*]. What's this?

WEE FARLEIGH. A madeleine. Small, rich gateau, baked in a shell-shaped tin.

FLORA. A what?

PEARL. A biscuit. Only better.

> *She eats it, takes another.* WEE FARLEIGH *serves tea.*

105

It is the secret of immortality. And what is immortality, but the fact of our common substance? One day, you and I and those daubs of paint [*the family portrait*] might trace our origins to a common ancestor, and that ancestor might turn out to be a mere... particle.

FLORA. "Remember man that thou art dust, and to dust thou shalt return."

PEARL. What's wrong, Doctor?

DR REID. Nothing. You reminded me of someone just now.

PEARL. Who? Father?

DR REID. No, no; someone I knew a very long time ago.

PEARL. Did she look like me?

DR REID. It was a he. And no, he didn't resemble you in the slightest – not outwardly – but I dare say the two of you might have struck up a friendship.

PEARL. We might even now. Is he still alive?

DR REID. In a manner of speaking, yes. He was, I confess, myself. Foolish –

PEARL. Not at all.

DR REID. Fanciful –

ACT II

PEARL. Seamus, you're blushing.

> *A beat. She's smiling at him. He returns the smile. Laughs. She joins in.*

DR REID. Pearl, I too heard that siren call from the bottomless well of deep time, for that is where our ultimate origins are to be found. And in my mind's eye, I gazed through that microscope of finer and finer distinctions until it seemed all was... one. But those hypnotic depths can paralyze the will. Cast your gaze forward, my friend. Science now calls upon us to stake out the boundaries; to etch boldly those lines between one species and another, lines which Myth and Religion have smudged, and which Nature has only sketchily indicated.

PEARL. Nature is an impressionist, then.

DR REID. And I would not have a Renoir on my wall for all the tea in China, for what do these Turners and Whistlers do? They glorify Nature's seductive pull back to the primordial swamp out of which we so recently crawled; a pull to which we are now more susceptible than ever. Pearl, when our great Queen Victoria was born, man could travel no more swiftly than the ancient Egyptians, by horse; now the country is traversed by trains, oceans are plied by steamships; there will soon be horseless carriages clogging the streets and flying machines crowding the heavens. Innoculations save lives, sanitation extends lives, humane laws protect the defective where once they'd have been cruelly cast out to perish. We are at an historic juncture. Thanks to our interventions, Nature no longer holds dominion over our survival; she has lost the power to select the fit and discard the unfit. It's up to us. We are, like it or not, *in locus Dei*.

PEARL. And what we are to do in God's place? How are we to know what God's work is?

DR REID. It is to forge an earthly paradise; to rouse the infant science of eugenics from its cradle; to engender a blueprint for the New Man: genetically pure, morally uncontaminated.

PEARL. To identify the cause of the ear. And eradicate it.

DR REID. Yes.

PEARL. As far as we know, there is nothing in the fossil record to indicate man's descent from dogs.

DR REID. There is not.

PEARL. Then, assuming the ear is canine, how can it be a throwback? If it were, one would expect it to be ape-like.

DR REID. All mammals share a common ancestor.

ACT II

PEARL. Wolves and primates diverged much later; thus if a human being exhibits a canine trait, the chance of it being atavistic is exceedingly slight.

DR REID. Point taken. Then we are left, merely, with a case of monstrous birth; singular, interesting, but... [*disappointed*] meaningless.

PEARL. Unless...

DR REID. Unless?

PEARL. Cast your gaze forward, my friend. Might it not be an emergent characteristic? Signalling the rise of a new species.

A beat. The holy grail.

DR REID. Nature's most closely guarded secret.

PEARL. The inner workings of life itself. Exposed.

A beat.

DR REID. Marry me, Pearl, and I will take you to the source of the ear.

PEARL. So you do know where it is from.

DR REID. Yes.

PEARL. And you will take me there. To the village on the Caucasian steppes.

DR REID. I will take you to the ends of the earth. As man and wife.

A beat.

PEARL. Seamus... [*suddenly*] What's that smell?

FLORA. What smell?

PEARL. It's an overpowering stench of... paint.
[*Covers her mouth.*]

DR REID. Pearl –

PEARL. I'm fine. I felt a bit queasy this morning,
but I'm better now.

FLORA. Queasy?

DR REID. This morning?

FLORA. Is it your woman's time?

PEARL. Flora! I'm perfectly fine, [*as though suddenly recovered*] in fact I'm longing for lunch-
eon.

FLORA. Wee Farleigh's fixed a lovely... French
thing.

WEE FARLEIGH *exits.*

PEARL. Winkles.

FLORA. Winkles?

PEARL. I must have them, tell Wee Farleigh – or
no, I'll tell him myself.

PEARL *exits.*

FLORA. What's the matter with the lass? Queasy one moment, craving winkles the next, it's almost as though she were... Seamus, you haven't!

DR REID. Of course not, Flora.

FLORA. Then...?

DR REID. It is just possible that Pearl is exhibiting early signs of a psychosomatic ailment.

FLORA. ... How did she catch it?

DR REID. Dear Flora. There is every reason to hope that Pearl's symptoms will disappear once she is wed, and at last free from the shadow of her well-intentioned father. [*Taking her hand.*] I'm sorry if I was hard on you, old friend. I must be cruel to be kind.

FLORA. Seamus, how do you aim to keep your promise?

DR REID. What promise?

FLORA. You said you'd show her where you got the ear.

DR REID. Pearl can be made to know what, without having to know who.

> DR REID *exits.* FLORA *peers at the painting. Sniffs the air. Exits.* VICTOR *rolls over. The scene changes around him. Walls dissolve. Sound of the sea, a woman singing "Au Claire de La Lune".* THE BRIDE *appears. She*

is pregnant. They don't speak, but we hear their voices as ambient sound.

THE BRIDE. Look what I found at the top of the Caucasian steps.

VICTOR. Aonaibh ri cheile.

THE BRIDE. I would, but it's too blurry.

> *Sound of a woman crying. The full moon rises.* THE BRIDE *turns her head and lifts her veil to reveal a Jackal ear.* PUPPY *whimpers from off. The silhouette of* THE JACKAL *appears in the family portrait, accompanied by the drone of a bagpipe.*

Scene 6 The Drawing Room

Next morning. PEARL *lies, dishevelled on the couch, a cold cloth on her forehead.* VICTOR *enters, pristine and jaunty, in travelling clothes.*

VICTOR. Well, I'm off. Goodbye, Pearl.

PEARL. Victor – [*moving to sit up, but finding it advisable not to*].

VICTOR. You look like you're about to upthrow, shall I fetch a bucket?

PEARL. Don't you dare go off down to the pub again, you're terribly ill. Tell Wee Farleigh to bring me a basket of brioches. And a pickled egg.

ACT II

VICTOR. Don't worry, Pearl, I'm not off down the pub, I'm just off. I'm leaving. [*calling off*] Wee Far –

PEARL. Shush – wait – what? Why?

VICTOR. I've a good deal of work that needs avoiding. I may even begin not-writing my novel.

PEARL. You can do that here. We'll make you a garret as drafty and uncomfortable as you like.

VICTOR. My mind's made up.

PEARL. You're not planning to leap into the sea, Victor, promise me –

VICTOR [*jovial*]. I'm not deep enough for despair, Pearl, the most I can muster is a cheerful self-loathing. I promise to kill myself very, very slowly.

PEARL. You'll need money, if you wait a few weeks I'll be able to –

VICTOR. Thanks, but I'm a boyishly handsome, shite-talking Scotsman with a well-endowed mythopoetical faculty. A mirror for the folly of others, a delightful extra man at table. There's always men willing to stand me drinks, and women... well I'm no' proud of it.

PEARL. What about your phobia? What if you run into a dog?

VICTOR. I'm not convinced it's the dogs, Pearl. I think I'm allergic to this house. [*Sniffs, will he sneeze?*] So I'll take me chances. Besides, all the best artists have fits. If I can't have the talent, at least I'll have the temperament.

PEARL. Where will you go?

VICTOR. Australia? Canada? A lot of worthless young men do quite well out there.

PEARL [*fierce*]. Victor, this is my house and I damn well give you half. Don't go.

VICTOR. I love you, Pearl. [*a beat*] Good luck with the natural history. And the unnatural history. Thank you for the puppy. Sorry about the ear.

PEARL. So it was you.

VICTOR. It wasn't, but I'm willing to sign a blank cheque of apology.

PEARL. Well if it wasn't you, then who – ?

> DR REID *enters, carrying a bouquet of red flowers.*

DR REID. Good morning, Pearl, good morning Victor.

VICTOR [*congenial*]. Good morning, Dr Jekyll.

> PEARL *sits up, attempting to straighten her hair.*

Dr Reid. Don't get up, my dear.

Pearl. I must look a fright.

Dr Reid. You look lovely.

Victor. She looks like a dog's breakfast.

Dr Reid. Did you take the powders this morning as I prescribed?

Victor. I sold them to an itinerant drug fiend.

Dr Reid. How's the nausea?

Pearl. The nausea's fine, excellent.

Dr Reid. Good. No... cravings?

Pearl. None.

Victor. Shall I fetch a haggis with the brioches?

Dr Reid [*handing her the bouquet*]. These are for you.

Pearl. Oh, Dr Reid, they're lovely.

Victor. They're poppies.

Dr Reid. From my own garden.

> Flora *enters with a cup of herbal tea for* Pearl.

Flora. This brew always restored your mother when she was – [*sees the others*].

Victor. Auntie, farewell.

FLORA. You're never leaving us?

VICTOR. Duty calls, I've taken a commission in the Queen's Own Rifles.

DR REID. You have?

VICTOR. I've done no such thing.

PEARL *fends off nausea.*

FLORA. What is it, Pearl? Do you smell something? Is it the painting again?

VICTOR *sniffs the painting.*

PEARL. I'm perfectly well, if a tad forfochen; that woman kept me up half the nicht. Night.

FLORA. What woman?

PEARL. The woman weeping. I looked out my window but couldn't get a glimpse of her. A woman from the estate, no doubt; drunk and disorderly.

FLORA. I didna hear a woman.

PEARL. You must have.

VICTOR. You heard my dream, Pearl.

FLORA. You heard the banshee.

PEARL. The banshee?

FLORA. The banshee only sings to a chosen one.

VICTOR. Chosen for what?

FLORA. To receive a warnin' of the great change.

A beat.

PEARL. Menopause?

FLORA. When the banshee wails, it means that someone will soon cross over to the other side.

VICTOR. I dreamt it was your dream, Pearl.

PEARL. Shutup, Victor.

FLORA. Your ancestors are tryin' to tell you something.

VICTOR [*to* FLORA]. That's 'cause *you* never tell us *anything*.

DR REID. Pearl, a degree of correspondence in dreams is not unheard of. You are siblings, after all, and have recently shared the ordeal of your father's death, and the aftershock of his will.

PEARL. Thank you, Seamus.

VICTOR. It's "Seamus" now, is it? Since when?

PEARL. Victor. Doctor Reid has asked me to marry him.

A beat.

VICTOR [*to* DR REID]. I didn't hear you ask my permission.

PEARL. Don't be ridiculous, Victor.

VICTOR [*alarmed*]. Don't marry him, Pearl.

PEARL. I'll marry whom I please.

VICTOR. He's tryin' to creep into Father's shoes and your bed besides.

PEARL. You're disgusting.

VICTOR. He wants to wrap you in his formaldehyde embrace and put you in a jar on his laboratory shelf.

PEARL. If it wasn't for Dr Reid, you'd be walking about dead right now, he's your best friend in the world!

VICTOR. He's a corp-liftin' ghoul and he's bullied Auntie Flora into league with him! Has he given you a ring? Or has he got a different gift tucked away for you in his bag of tricks? Perhaps one of his magic potions he's been longing to prick you with! [*Snatching* DR REID*'s medical bag.*]

PEARL. Victor – !

VICTOR [*rifling it*]. Ha-ha! [*Holding up a scalpel.*] Performed any field surgery lately? As well to have it on hand in case you encounter a promising two-headed calf, eh?

DR REID. Victor, my boy, give me the scalpel.

ACT II

VICTOR [*dropping the bag, brandishing the scalpel, deadly earnest*]. Tell me the truth.

DR REID. I don't know what you –

VICTOR. The truth about my family! The "burden", the "horror"! I heard you on the attic stairs, there's not a corner of this house you've no' pissed in and defiled, tell me or I'll cut your throat!

PEARL [*enraged*]. I'll tell you the secret, Victor! It was your precious mother. She was mad, and it's coming out in you, and it would come out in my curs'ed progeny. Dr Reid wants to marry me to shield me from it; to be on hand when you spiral into the pit, so that you may rave within the confines of Belle Moral and not some forsaken madhouse!

VICTOR [*stricken*]. Is it true, Auntie?

> DR REID *prepares a needle.*

Was she mad? According to whom? To you, Doctor? And what did you do? Put her away in your asylum? Why? Did you want her for yourself? Did you have her? [*grief-stricken*] Did she die there?

DR REID [*approaching with needle*]. Victor, lad –

> VICTOR *slashes.* DR REID *jumps aside.*

FLORA. Victor, sweetheart –

119

VICTOR [*fending her off with the scalpel, furious*]. No!

> *He backs away and exits out the window.*

FLORA [*running after him*]. Victor – !

DR REID [*alarmed*]. Flora, no!

PEARL. Auntie!

FLORA. He's like to drown himself in truth this time – !

DR REID. We'll see that doesn't happen [*pulling the bell cord*] we'll send Wee Farleigh.

PEARL. Doctor... if I go mad –

DR REID. You won't –

PEARL. If I go mad I want you to promise me – [*covering her nose and mouth*] – I know you can't smell it. I know what's happening to me.

DR REID. My dear, you've been under a terrible strain –

PEARL [*controlling her terror*]. It's in me too – the flaw – and it will out. It's begun already.

> WEE FARLEIGH *enters.*

DR REID. Pearl –

> *She seizes* DR REID*'s hand and presses it against her belly.*

120

PEARL. You know what it is. I can see it in your
    eyes. Why won't you say?

FLORA. Pearl, you mustn't –

PEARL [*savage*]. You're not my mother! And you,
    Doctor, are not my father. While I am still
    lucid, in the time that remains to me, I in-
    tend to work. But I'll not parade myself as
    an obscene and bloated curiosity – you see,
    Doctor, I am still in possession of my facul-
    ties, able to diagnose myself, even if you
    won't. [*fighting nausea*] Promise me that
    when my condition becomes apparent, you
    will operate.

FLORA. Operate?

PEARL. You will perform a complete hysterectomy.

DR REID. Pearl –

PEARL [*commanding*]. Promise me!

DR REID. I promise.

PEARL. But neither Victor nor I, no matter how
    acute our condition, is ever to be committed
    to an asylum.

DR REID. I promise.

PEARL. We're to live here at Belle Moral, and Aunt-
    ie is to be provided for.

DR REID. I promise.

A beat.

PEARL. I'll marry you, Seamus.

FLORA [*repeating under her breath, as though praying*]. *Deanum dhuit eolas, gu casgadh beum sula. Air na naodha conair, air na naodha conachair, air na naodha coilechinn, air naodha ban senga sith.* [pron. Jaynum hoed olas, g'càskar bayum sohluh. Air na nuh-ee conn-er, air na nuh-ee conna-hair, air na nuh-ee colla-hin, air nuhee banna sheng-ah shee] [trans: I make for thee a charm to check the evil eye. Against the nine paths, against the nine tumults, against the nine crafty wiles, against the nine slender women of the underworld]

> PEARL *sways on her feet, falls,* WEE FARLEIGH *catches her.* FLORA *puts the tea cup to* PEARL*'s lips.* PEARL *straightens, takes the cup and hurls the contents at the painting. Thunder. It begins to rain.* PEARL *exits.* FLORA f*ollows her.* WEE FARLEIGH *awaits instructions.*

DR REID. Send for the Justice of the Peace.

ACT III

Scene 1 The Attic

That night. Rain throughout the the following scenes. Candle light. A single cot. A wash basin. A small crucifix on the wall. THE CREATURE *huddles in the worn tartan shawl that obscures its face.* DR REID *is formally dressed.*

DR REID. Come. There's a good girl.

> THE CREATURE *is motionless.* DR REID *takes something from his pocket, crouches, gently holds out his hand.*

Have a sweet. Go ahead. [*drawing closer, friendly*] I'm not going to hurt you.

> THE CREATURE *lunges, taking a ferocious swipe at him with its bare hands, and swiftly retreats to a crouch.* DR REID *falls back, clutching his neck.*

Damn you!

> *He is bleeding. He backs away cautiously, reaching for his medical bag.*

Scene 2 Pearl's Bedroom

PEARL, *in travelling tweeds, brushes her hair back into a severe bun.* FLORA *enters with a wedding gown.* PEARL *stares.*

FLORA. You'll only be wed once. Please, pet.

PEARL. Has Victor come home yet?

> FLORA *shakes her head, no. Hides her face in the gown.*

Scene 3 The Painting

Thunder. Lightening plays upon the canvas. The colours have begun to run at the centre, revealing a shadowy figure.

Scene 4 The Drawing Room

DR REID *waits in his finery. His neck is bandaged. He stares at the painting. Approaches, about to touch it, when* PEARL *enters, wearing the wedding gown and veil. She lifts the veil.* DR REID *is over-whelmed at the sight: she is beautiful.*

PEARL [*all but paralyzed with grief*]. My brother is dead, Seamus.

DR REID. No, my dear, we'll find him, I promise you.

PEARL. The sea has him. She's rocking him gently now.

DR REID. Hush.

PEARL [*wiping tears*]. She loves him. She loves us all.

DR REID. You are beautiful, Pearl. More beautiful, even, than your mother. [*Holding out his hand.*] Come. There's a good girl.

> *He is about to take her hand when* WEE FARLEIGH *enters.*

WEE FARLEIGH. The Justice of the Peace has arrived.

PEARL. What are you doing here? Why aren't you out looking for my brother?

WEE FARLEIGH. Your brother – ?

DR REID [*to* WEE FARLEIGH]. That will be all –

FLORA [*from off*]. Help!!

PEARL. Victor!

FLORA [*entering*]. She's dead! Lord help us, Seamus, she's – !

DR REID. Hush, Flora – !

FLORA. I canna wake her!

PEARL. Who? Who is dead?

FLORA. Och, I told ee, Seamus, I warned ee, the banshee niver lies – !

DR REID. She's alive, I tell you!

PEARL. What is going on in this house?!

DR REID. Pearl –

PEARL. Tell me!

DR REID. Wait until we are wed, I beseech you.

PEARL. Why?

DR REID. Because...

PEARL. Because it is a horror.

DR REID. Because it is a gift. My gift to you.

FLORA. Seamus – !

PEARL. Show me this instant. Or leave my sight.

> *He holds out his hand. She takes it. Thunder. They exit. FLORA goes to follow but turns back.*

FLORA. Why have you given up the search?

WEE FARLEIGH. What search, Miss?

FLORA. Did Dr Reid not ask you to find young Master MacIsaac?

WEE FARLEIGH. No, Miss. Miss, the Justice of Peace is waiting in the conservatory. Shall I offer him some refreshment?

Scene 5 The Attic

PEARL, DR REID *at her side, gazes at* THE CREATURE *who lies, immobile on the cot, dressed in a white nightgown.* THE CREATURE'*s long hair is spread out around her, the tartan shawl lies discarded on the floor.* PEARL *goes to approach, but hesitates.*

DR REID. Go ahead. It is quite safe.

PEARL. Who is she?

DR REID. Pearl, approach the subject. Closer examination may prompt you to revise your question.

> PEARL *goes closer. She sees something on one side of* THE CREATURE'*s head and is startled, then drawn in.*

Ay. "What" is she? That is the question you and I shall dedicate our lives to answering. Oh, Pearl; I worship you.

> FLORA *enters.* THE CREATURE *stirs.*

You see, Flora? She is not dead. Merely sedated.

FLORA. Why?

DR REID. She's my patient. I'm treating her.

> PEARL, *speechless, smooths the hair back from the other side of the woman's face to reveal a scar in place of an ear. She looks to* DR REID.

I'll answer your questions, my darling, every one. Come away now, the Justice of the Peace is waiting –

127

FLORA. No he's not. I sent him away.

DR REID. Have you taken leave of your senses?

FLORA. You never told Wee Farleigh to go out after Victor. You left the lad to wander all alone, weeping and raging, and on such a night, why? When you know what can happen?

DR REID. Pearl, your brother is more histrionic than hysterical, the best thing for it is to ignore him.

FLORA [*to* PEARL]. She's your sister.

DR REID. Flora – !

FLORA. She is your sister, Pearl, your flesh and blood, I wanted to tell you, but Dr Reid –

DR REID [*icy*]. As I recall, Flora, we agreed –

FLORA [*outraged, to* DR REID]. Fiend!

DR REID [*forced calm, to* PEARL]. My dearest girl. There is no reason why this need alter, in the slightest degree, the course of your life. Look away now and we shall never mention this night again.

> VICTOR *and* WEE FARLEIGH *enter.* VICTOR *is soaked.*

FLORA [*seeing* VICTOR *safe*]. Oh thank God.

ACT III

> Victor *sees* The Creature. *His breathing becomes slightly laboured.*

Pearl. She's our sister, Victor.

> Victor *draws near. He sees what* Pearl *saw. His breathing calms.*

Flora [*gentle*]. Victor, sweetheart, she's your twin.

> *A beat.*

Pearl. Am I to understand that... she has been here, under this roof –

Flora. No, no –

Dr Reid. No, your father sent her away –

Flora. For your sakes –

Dr Reid. The child was placed in a home.

Pearl. What "home"?

Flora [*making excuses*]. A decent one, in the north–

Dr Reid [*in contrast to* Flora, *determined not to mince words*]. A home for lunatics.

Pearl. Is she a lunatic?

Dr Reid. She is not *compos mentis* in the usual sense, but nor is she clinically mad.

Pearl. Then why was she in a mad house?

Flora. Your father wanted her cared for... else-where.

DR REID. It was a diagnosis of convenience. And I made it, God forgive me, out of loyalty to Ramsay. But you can imagine the calibre of care.

FLORA. It was respectable haim, Young Farleigh visited –

DR REID. How often did you visit, Flora?

> *A beat.* FLORA *is too ashamed to answer.* DR REID *addresses* PEARL.

A remote and antiquated facility designed solely for the warehousing of the blighted, the delinquent, the feeble-minded, mad, and otherwise unwanted members of "respectable" families. Ay, Flora, you've taken "good care" of the children. She's lucky to be alive. [*to* VICTOR *and* PEARL] She's here now only because your aunt ran out of money, [*to* FLORA] isn't that so? But now that she is here, I vow upon my honour that I shall spend the rest of my life, restoring purpose to hers.

VICTOR. What's wrong with her?

DR REID. She was born like that.

VICTOR. No, why doesn't she wake up? You've drugged her, why?

DR REID. Would you rather see her in a strait-jacket?

PEARL. Did Mother... see her?

FLORA *weeps*.

DR REID. Your mother wanted to keep the child. Régine was... tender-hearted. I tried to convince Ramsay. I thought I could heal the poor thing – or at least remove the deformity. And I made a start. But Ramsay changed his mind before I could finish.

PEARL. She was an infant, then, when you operated?

DR REID. Of course; infants, like animals, feel no pain, but Ramsay took it into his head that the creature was suffering. Then your mother passed away and... [*struggling; it is difficult for him to talk about Régine, and the painful events of those days*]. I hadn't the heart to continue even if your father had permitted it, so I... laid my research to rest, along with Régine's dear... dear memory. But Pearl, your passion has rekindled my own. And I'm glad I did not proceed with the crude methods of my youth, for I realize now that her anatomy conceals treasures beyond the reach of a mere scalpel. You were right: she is an original; a real-life chimera; a brave new world, undiscovered, unclaimed. Oh Pearl, she has so much to teach us: about what we are; where we come from; where we are going and where we must not go. We stand poised to breach Nature's last

131

frontier. Within our grasp is the knowledge and the power: to select the best of Earth's bounty; to combine what is there, to create what is not, to make a heaven of this hell. To chart Utopia in our time. The work begins here. With her offspring.

VICTOR. Her "offspring"?

DR REID. What I propose is standard laboratory procedure. Painless, humane –

VICTOR. Hers and who else's? Yours? The puppy's?

DR REID. You're a disgrace.

FLORA. You're a disgrace! And so am I, we've had no right –

DR REID. I have a duty! Pearl, I would not harm her in any way, why should I wish to? She is a gift.

FLORA. Ramsay forbade you to touch another hair on her head.

DR REID [*furious*]. Ramsay wanted to drown it!

FLORA. If that's true, it only shows he didna want the poor creature to suffer.

DR REID. He didn't want his *pride* to suffer! Ask Young Farleigh. Ramsay told him to put it in a sack and throw it into the sea. [*blazing*] I saved it! It's mine!

ACT III

> *A beat.* THE CREATURE *awakens. Sits up. It is a young woman.* DR REID *draws back.* PEARL *approaches.*

PEARL. What is your name?

DR REID. It doesn't have a name.

PEARL. Speak, child.

FLORA. She canna speak, pet.

PEARL. What is your name?

> *A beat.*

YOUNG WOMAN. Claire.

> *A beat.*

PEARL. I think you'd better leave now, Doctor.

DR REID. Pearl –

PEARL [*calm*]. Get out of my house.

> DR REID *takes his medical bag and exits.* PEARL *smooths the hair from* CLAIRE'*s face, to reveal a tall red canine ear. She strokes it.* VICTOR *picks up the tartan shawl, buries his face in it and inhales.*

Did Mother go mad, Flora?

FLORA. No, pet. She was just terribly, terribly sad. She walked into the sea.

Scene 6 The Drawing Room

Four months later. MR ABBOTT *waits, briefcase in hand.* YOUNG FARLEIGH *is asleep in the chair under the worn tartan shawl,* PUPPY *tucked by his side. The family portrait hangs once more over the mantle piece, the space between* PEARL *and* VICTOR *now revealed to contain an infant with the ears of a puppy.* ABBOTT *squints at the portrait.* PEARL *enters. Her hair is down, her flowing garments anticipate Vanessa Bell, and are particularly generous about the midriff.*

PEARL. Ah, Mr Abbott.

ABBOTT. Good afternoon, Miss MacIsaac.

PEARL. Have you brought the documents?

ABBOTT. I have, Miss. [*a beat*] If you will permit me to say so, Miss MacIsaac, you are looking particularly well this afternoon.

PEARL. Thank you, Mr Abbott, I'm feeling particularly well.

ABBOTT. I had the good luck to attend a lecture yesterday evening, and have taken the liberty of bringing you a transcript which I venture to hope may excite your interest. [*Hands her a sheaf of paper.*]

PEARL [*reading*]. "Fossils of All Kinds, Digested into a Method Suitable to Their Mutual Relation and Affinity".

ACT III

She kisses Mr Abbott. *It's a long kiss.*

Mr Abbott, would you consent to be in a photograph?

Abbott [*speechless*].

Pearl. Good. Please join Auntie Flora in the conservatory.

> *He bows and exits, blindly. The clock strikes three.* Pearl *turns toward the entrance, expectant.* Dr Reid *enters.*

Dr Reid. Hello, Pearl.

Pearl. Hello, Doctor. Thank you for coming.

Dr Reid [*slight bow*].

Pearl. Dr Reid, I have something of a delicate nature to tell you; and something of vital import, for which I must ask –

Dr Reid. Don't ask. There is no need. My dear, I have already forgiven you. I am a doctor; I, of all men, ought to have been unsurprised by your reaction that fearful night. It is I who am at fault for having allowed these several months to pass in silence, but I have been much in demand abroad – nay, 'tisn't only that; I confess my pride was wounded. Still, when I received your invitation to call today, any trace of rancour melted away, so let us speak no more of it.

A beat.

PEARL. I'm pregnant.

> *A beat.* VICTOR *enters carrying* PEARL*'s camera with its hood and tripod. He wears a velvet cape and vest, a ruffled shirt and tight pants. He deposits the equipment, exits.* DR REID *notices the family portrait.* VICTOR *returns with* CLAIRE *by the hand. She is dressed as a cowgirl, with holsters and six-guns. Her hair is up, displaying her ear to advantage.* VICTOR *positions her on the couch and sets up the camera.* DR REID *stares.* PEARL *is pleasant and business-like.*

> [*to* DR REID] So you see, it throws a bit of a wrench into the inheritance.

DR REID. I beg your pardon?

PEARL. Father's will. Bars me from bearing children.

DR REID. Pearl, dearest. Do you not recall, you yourself had the presence of mind to diagnose your condition. I sought, mistakenly I now see, to shield you from the truth, but the fact is, the power of repressed emotions has exacted a psychosomatic toll –

PEARL. – my womb is in revolt against the proviso of my father's will –

DR REID. – such that your pregnancy is, in reality–

PEARL. Hysterical.

DR REID. Yes.

PEARL. No. At least not any more. Whatever was ailing me – hysterical, fantastical, or perfectly logical – it was certainly a conception of my mind, but I can assure you such is no longer the case.

A beat.

DR REID. You mean to say... ? Victor, at this juncture it would behoove a gentleman to leave a lady alone with her physician.

VICTOR. Ay, it would.

He plunks down on the couch next to CLAIRE. *They eat shortbread and watch.*

DR REID. My dear, who has done this to you? I'll have him clapped in irons.

PEARL. I really can't say, Doctor.

A beat.

DR REID. How many men have there been?

PEARL. Need there have been any?

DR REID. Well how, otherwise, do you explain your pregnancy?

VICTOR. A lady needn't explain.

PEARL. No, but I shall. Perhaps it is parthenogenic.

DR REID. Human asexual reproduction? Impossible.

PEARL. "Man can believe the impossible, but man can never believe the improbable."

VICTOR. Who said that? The pope?

PEARL. Oscar Wilde.

DR REID. Apart from a rare species of lizard, parthenogenic reproduction in multi-celled creatures is confined to the class of worms and religious myth.

PEARL. Perhaps I have diversified successfully.

VICTOR. She was down winkling on the shore when she met a fellow with great tall ears and a long snout. Loaded with baked goods, he was.

PEARL. Victor dreamt I was impregnated by a psychopomp.

DR REID. You claim to have had congress with the Egyptian God of the Underworld?

VICTOR. Not only that, she cured my phobia.

PEARL. I merely ventured that Victor, via his fits, may have subconsciously registered a warning: to wit, if we refuse to acknowledge kinship, not only with the mythic dog, but with all matter; if we resist the central truth of evolution –

ACT III

DR REID. I am a child of the Enlightenment, I resist nothing that is rational, I believe in evolution, along with the rest of the civilized world.

PEARL. The civilized world behaves least as if it did believe. For all our scientific pieties, we still organize our societies as though we alone had been created in the image of a god in whom we profess no longer to believe. We have slain our brother, Abel, and who was he? Did he walk on two legs, or four? Did he creep, or swim, or fly? If we fail to recognize our true nature, we shall conduct our lives according to criteria that are divorced from matter – from our mother – Earth. If we behave as gods – warring, feasting and plundering – then, like gods, are we doomed to disappear in a twilight of our own making? Perhaps Victor was no more "hysterical" than Cassandra when she prophesied the fall of Troy. Lucky for her she didn't live today, she'd be walking about short of a uterus by now.

DR REID. Pearl, I understand your reluctance to confess... multiple indiscretions. But I fear you may be suffering from a more serious malady.

PEARL. What is that?

DR REID. I cannot, in all decency, speak the word. Be assured there is hope that, with timely surgical intervention –

VICTOR. He thinks you're a nymphomaniac.

PEARL. Really, Doctor? I've always wondered what they looked like.

VICTOR. Just my luck I'd finally meet a nympho and she'd turn out to be me sister.

DR REID. Pearl, I'm still willing to marry you.

> MR ABBOTT *enters dressed as a Highland warrior, his face streaked blue, still wearing his pince nez and carrying his briefcase.*

ABBOTT. Good afternoon, Doctor.

DR REID [*to* PEARL]. Is this the man?

VICTOR. "Crucify him!"

PEARL. Mr Abbott, the documents, please.

VICTOR. Look lively, Lorenzo, we're due at the asylum at half six.

DR REID. The asylum?

VICTOR. We're going curling with the lunatics. They've got up a bonspiel.

DR REID. Pearl –

PEARL. I've no plans to marry at present, Doctor, thank you all the same.

DR REID. You realize that in the absence of an heir, Belle Moral must revert to the Kirk. I am not a rich man, but I am far from poor and I pledge to provide for you all.

> MR ABBOTT *hands* PEARL *a legal-size document from his briefcase.*

PEARL. Thank you, Mr Abbott.

DR REID. You'll be out in the street, the lot of you. Who will you depend upon then, eh? Your brother? He isn't fit to black my boots. Your aunt? How will you live on the few pennies she'd eke out as a seamstress or washerwoman? That leaves you, Pearl, and whatever special talents you may have discovered of late.

> PEARL *slaps him.*

Quite right. Forgive me. Marry me.

VICTOR. But Doctor, there is an heir.

DR REID. Where?

PEARL. Claire.

> FLORA *enters dressed as Cleopatra.*

FLORA. I'm ready, Pearl, how do you want me? [*sees* DR REID, *stops*]

VICTOR. Auntie, you are *ravissanti*.

PEARL [*to* DR REID]. My sister is quite competent. Despite twenty-seven years of privation she has, in a matter of months, learned to eat with a knife and fork, mastered the alphabet, and ceased to growl.

DR REID. She can't inherit.

PEARL. Why not? You said yourself she's not a lunatic.

DR REID. She's an animal!

FLORA. We're all of us animals.

DR REID. You won't find a physician with a scrap of integrity willing to certify her human much less sane.

VICTOR. That leaves you, then.

DR REID. I'll sign nothing. In the eyes of the law, this creature does not even exist, she hasn't so much as a birth certificate.

> *Realizes what he has said even as* PEARL *produces a second document.*

That was Ramsay's idea. He forbade me to register her birth, he –

PEARL. In the eyes of the law, you as attending physician were responsible for registering the child's birth.

ACT III

ABBOTT [*reading from a law book through his pince nez*]. "It shall be the duty of every qualified medical practitioner attending at the birth of any child, to give notice thereof forthwith to the Division Registrar of the Division in which the child was born – "

DR REID. I am aware of the law.

ABBOTT. "Any physician making a false statement – "

DR REID. I said –

ABBOTT. " – as to the cause of *death* of any person shall be subject to discipline by the Medical Council of – "

DR REID. This is my recompense? This, my due?

PEARL. You falsified Mother's death certificate to conceal her suicide.

DR REID. For you. For the sake of your family name–

ABBOTT. " – shall, on summary conviction therefor, be liable for every such offence to a penalty of – "

DR REID. Enough!

> DR REID *signs the documents.*

Where's your integrity now, eh Abbott? Where in your legal lexicon does blackmail appear as a just remedy?

ABBOTT. See under "humane".

DR REID. See under "sex".

> WEE FARLEIGH *enters as Pan, with horns, furry legs and pan pipes.*

You are not well, Pearl. And what you nourish in your womb harbours the taint of your own forbears along with the moral degeneracy of some stray male.

> *He looks from* WEE FARLEIGH *to* MR ABBOTT. *They look at one another then at* DR REID.

PEARL. What I carry, is a gift.

DR REID. When you see it you will beg me to take it from you.

PEARL [*going to her camera*]. Are we ready? Gather round, now.

> *They gather on and around the couch.*

Young Farleigh. [*loudly*] Young Farleigh!

DR REID. You're mad.

PEARL [*unable to rouse him*]. Well, gather round Young Farleigh then.

> *They do.*

DR REID. What are you doing?

PEARL. I'm taking a family photograph.

DR REID. This is your notion of family? This is not a family, this is... a menagerie.

PEARL. The tree of life is a family tree and we are all part of it.

DR REID. Even him? [YOUNG FARLEIGH.]

PEARL. Even you, Doctor. Would you care to be in the picture?

DR REID. He'd've killed your precious sister. He was on the point of casting her from the cliff when I stopped him.

PEARL. But he hadn't yet, had he?

DR REID. Nay, but –

PEARL. So we'll never know.

DR REID. *He* knows.

PEARL. He doesn't. He hopes he would not have. But he doesn't know.

DR REID. You think he's atoned for that? How? By bringing her sweets in the asylum?

PEARL. He taught her her name.

DR REID. And that exonerates him?

PEARL. No. But it's the best we've got.

FLORA. I don't know that we're any of us fit to cast the first stone. Heaven will judge him.

VICTOR. He's coming back in his next life as a winkle. [*to* PEARL] Tell him to stop looking at me like that.

PEARL. Who?

VICTOR. Pan. [*to* WEE FARLEIGH] Pick on him, he's the one wearin' the skirt.

ABBOTT. It is a *kilt*, sir.

DR REID. Pearl, how do you propose to live? An unmarried woman with an illegitimate offspring, surrounded by a pack of lunatics, sodomites, and vegetarians.

PEARL. I am a scientist. I shall observe and document us. Belle Moral shall be my laboratory and we, my subjects.

DR REID. But you're part of the experiment.

PEARL. Aren't we all.

DR REID. You're not dispassionate.

PEARL. True. As it turns out I am terribly, terribly passionate.

DR REID. Your results will be corrupted. You cannot be both an observer and participant.

PEARL. I cannot but be both. "Observation is participation".

VICTOR. Who said that?

ACT III

PEARL. No one; but someone really ought to. Was I to work and dwell at your side, never knowing my true relation to the subject?

DR REID. Knowing who she was would have hindered your ability to discover what she is. What is the good of such knowledge?

PEARL. "Knowledge is power" said Francis Bacon. I too am a child of the Enlightenment.

DR REID. I fear you are its bastard.

PEARL. Was it rational to deprive me of the crucial fact?

DR REID. A fact that would have destroyed your objectivity.

PEARL. What is objectivity but the ability to consider every influence on our powers of observation? Facts, uprooted, can tell us only so much. A fact out of context is like a fish on a slab, inexplicable without water.

VICTOR. Like an ear in a jar, inexplicable without a head.

PEARL. Facts do not float in sterile solitude, they are embedded in reality, tainted with everyday life, stained with history; inextricable, like Darwin's web. How am I to know Claire and other marvels of nature as ordinary as a dust mote, if I do not admit to being part of that exquisitely, well-nigh infinitely, complex web? The remains of Julius Ceasar may be in that speck of dust. I shall be in that speck of dust one day. [*ambushed emotionally*] We are all here so briefly. Awake, for a moment. Unique, for a moment. Able to look and to love, for a moment. And then we return. To the generosity of this universe and its great making power. That is love. And nothing, not even the merest particle, reveals itself without it.

A beat.

ABBOTT. I have seen the face of God in a three hundred thousand year old trilobite.

A beat.

PEARL. Seamus, you look at us and see an incoherent jumble. I look and see affinities. Patterns.

VICTOR. A story.

PEARL. That's right. A plot. You're probably right, Seamus, we're probably quite a bad idea, really. We don't matter a great deal, we're on the fringes; of empire, of science, art and culture. We cannot even claim the weight of oppression that might yield a diamond eons from now. But perhaps, simply by thinking our thoughts and living our lives with passionate curiosity and unreasonable kindness, we do our part in the slow universal accumulation of – of critical mass, to coin a phrase – that crystallizes in true discovery.

FLORA. Pearl, it's nigh on four o'clock, your friends will be faimished, come Wee Farleigh and help me –

PEARL [*going for her camera*]. Don't you dare move, either of you.

FLORA. Your sister's faint with hunger, look at her.

PEARL. Of course she's half-starved, Victor's turned her into a vegetarian.

VICTOR. How can you talk of kindness, Pearl, and still eat other animals?

PEARL. Don't start, Victor.

VICTOR. You started it.

PEARL. I didna – !   VICTOR. Did – !

FLORA. I've a lovely leg of lamb, you're all to stay; and for the vegetablists, we've a... what's it called, Wee Farleigh?

WEE FARLEIGH. A medley of beans. Baked savoury squash. A casserole of wild champignons and nuts. A milles-feuilles of goat cheese, grilled aubergine, slow-roasted tomato mousse and toasted garlic on a bed of kelp. And for dessert: chocolate éclaires.

PEARL. The éclaires are for everyone, surely.

VICTOR. No, you get a black-pudding for dessert.

PEARL. Seamus, will you stay to tea?

> *A beat.*

DR REID. You are stubborn, clannish and benight-
ed. An apple falls from a tree and you do
not shout, "Eureka!", you eat the apple. You
have no real conscience, only sentiment:
you'd save the one to the detriment of the
many, and call it "kindness". You lack the
mental rigour for true kindness. You shrink
from inconvenient facts, preferring a retreat
to your hot-house of exotic half-truths; your
ramshackle relativism; your primordial
swamp; your bog, your blur. You haven't the
strength to withstand the whirlwind, or the
unflinching gaze required to see into it. One
look at the face of God and you would be an-
nihilated. It is dearly to be hoped that you
occupy an evolutionary cul-de-sac. Otherwise, heaven help us all.

> *Exit,* DR REID. PEARL *unwinds a cord with
> a small plunger from the camera and runs
> it to where the company is assembled for
> the photo. She holds the plunger and as-
> sumes her position in the photo line-up.*

PEARL. Ready? [*About to press the plunger.*] And —

CLAIRE. Ainaibh ri chelie.

> YOUNG FARLEIGH *wakes up.*

ACT III

PEARL. What does that mean?

YOUNG FARLEIGH. 'Tis Gaelic.

VICTOR. I know "'tis Gaelic" –

FLORA. It's your mother's clan motto –

CLAIRE. It means: "unite".

> PEARL *presses the plunger and the camera*
> *responds with a poof and a flash. Curtain.*
> PUPPY *barks.*

Afterword

by Ann-Marie MacDonald

Belle Moral: A Natural History has its origins in
an earlier play of mine called *The Arab's Mouth*,
and the story of its evolution is also the story of a
creative relationship. *The Arab's Mouth* was first
produced in 1990 by Toronto's Factory Theatre and
its then-artistic director, Jackie Maxwell. An interesting sidebar – and natural history is all about
the sidebars – is that, at the time, I nurtured hopes
that one day the play might be programmed by the
Shaw Festival; this, owing to my passion for the
period, as well as my enduring regard for the Festival itself, then under the direction of Christopher
Newton. Alas, the mandate had yet to be expanded
to include works such as mine that were set but
not written during Shaw's lifetime – just as well,
for *The Arab's Mouth* had some critical evolutionary transformations to undergo before it became
Belle Moral.

   After *The Arab's Mouth* premiered, I knew
that it was not quite finished and, in keeping with
my experience as a playwright and collaborator, I
fully expected to return to it. I got distracted, how-

ever, by another project which I thought would be a play but turned out to be a novel. *Fall On Your Knees* developed many of the themes and images that I had touched on in *The Arab's Mouth*, and I came to see the play as a progenitor – or, to change metaphors, as a kind of sketch book for the novel. Years went by and I sought to lay to rest the little voice at the back of my mind insisting, "What about me?" *The Arab's Mouth* had become a ghost that would not rest, and no amount of fiction, or indeed other theatre work, would quiet it. Thus, when Jackie Maxwell invited me to revisit the piece, I was completely delighted and my initial inner response was, "No." Writing is hard. Rewriting is harder. And I was scared to look that deeply into my creative past, having never glanced at the script in all those intervening years. What would I find upon re-entering that abandoned house? Would the ghosts be angry? Spoiling for a fight? Or in the mood for a party? And what would my much younger self have to say to me now, an experienced writer striding in to turn it all upside down?

The first step was to read the play again after almost fourteen years. I did so, looking and listening for one thing – a heartbeat. There is a good reason why certain ghosts refuse to rest: they're not dead. There was indeed a heartbeat. A strong one. I was put in mind of a young race horse, all bony, and pounding with vitality, panting with the passion to run, bursting from the starting gate in all directions at once. It was all over the map, but it was alive.

I did much more work on the script than I, or I think Jackie, expected. Characters and elements of plot that I had once thought of as structurally and thematically integral went the way of the demolition crew without a tremor, clearing the way for new characters as well as new – if certainly fewer – story elements. A great deal had happened in the world and in my life as an artist since 1990, and my world-view had grown. Whereas *The Arab's Mouth* was an almost truculent assertion of the primacy of the irrational and the relativistic, *Belle Moral* reaches out in two directions to reconcile the extremes of rationalism and romanticism, in an attempt to re-envision and to articulate afresh those core Enlightenment values that engendered the freedom and equality that we take for granted at our peril. Today, the forces of fundamentalism threaten to undo that civilized and precious mess we call democracy, substituting simple answers and ruthless solutions in the place of plurality and debate, promoting superstition and prejudice over curiosity and courage. The Scopes Trial is being replayed in North American schools even as real-life chimeras are being created in labs – and moral vacuums – around the world; this mixture of backward thinking and highly sophisticated technology is potentially explosive.

But I'm essentially a comedian. Which is to say, an informed, jaded, jaundiced, optimist. There may be unhappy endings to stories, but all stories are happy, because as long as there are stories, there is hope. If even one person – or indeed, creature – is able to emerge from the rubble of our own making to say, "I remember what happened. Listen, and I'll tell you," that's a happy ending. Bearing witness can be just that: the carrying of a heavy load that eventually must be shared. As long as there is one ancient, flea-bitten, parched and starving mariner able to stagger up to a wedding party and tell his or her tale, there is compassion – that insight which makes the tale intelligible and is the progenitor of imagination. And imagination in turn, if it is not Dr Frankenstein's longed-for spark of life itself, is certainly the spark of civilization.

A Note for Practitioners

Belle Moral: A Natural History is a dark but redemptive comedy. At a narrative level, it is a story of family secrets come to light. It is also the story of the birth and evolution of ideas, and of ways of seeing, and living in, the world. As such, it is truly a play of morals. Stylistically there is fun to be had with its Gothic references, but the tone ought never to stray into pastiche or melodrama. That said, the stakes are high and, even in calmer moments, a sense of urgency is never far below the surface. These characters think quickly and speak articulately. They formulate their thoughts in the moment, and they enjoy argument.

Victor's lust for life extends to a revelling in his own "romantic martyrdom" – even when he is pouting, he does so with enthusiasm and is never depressive. His geniality, mischievous sarcasm and hell-bent good humour all serve to buoy him up over a well of grief. When that grief splashes up in the first act, and then when it boils over at the end of the second act, it is sudden, genuine and passionate.

Pearl protects herself emotionally with her arch tone and severe attitude toward Victor in particular and weakness in general, but beneath her controlled exterior is a deep love for her brother and unresolved grief at the loss of her mother and the remoteness of her father. If Victor is given to sudden swings between laughter and tears, Pearl switches just as rapidly between "cool" rationalism and white-hot rage.

Dr Reid is a reasonable man who embodies much of what was considered humane and progressive at the time. Indeed, some of his more odious views are still culturally dominant in ways that we might be reluctant to admit, while others are genuinely sound both morally and intellectually. His is the story of a man who is seduced by a second chance; of good intentions gone awry; of the subtle, and crucial, relationship between knowledge and power; and of the very different meanings – or species – of love. Dr Reid is the hero of his own story, a good and ethical man to the end, in his own eyes.

Flora is deceptively dotty on the surface, and fearless at the core. Her "dottiness" is an effect of her good-natured impulse to nurture her loved-ones, combined with her effort to keep track of all the lies and secrets in the family. With her hybrid belief system she is actually more open-minded than many other more sophisticated souls. One imagines her and Einstein chatting together quite happily. She is motivated by love for her family, but that love is tainted by a guilt that serves to distort her judgment until the final act.

Scene changes are, among other things, an opportunity for the Underworld to assert its presence in the person of the Anubis figure. In the first scene he claims the Bride for the Underworld, and by the third act he is waiting patiently for the chance to claim the Creature/Claire. It should be noted that the Bride is a ghostly evocation of Régine who has been searching the Underworld for her lost child, while hoping not to find her there.

Puppy, in the original production, was "played" by a puppet, specially constructed from a taxidermy mould, painted, and finished with fur. The head and tail detached, and he was operated by the actor playing The Bride/Creature/Claire, in a puppetry style reminiscent of that used in Japanese theatre.

By the end of the play, the world has changed. Gothic shadows have given way to the light of day, corsets disappear, and conformity is knocked aside by a deadly serious playfulness. For a moment, the horizon is unclouded. It is only a matter of time, however, before Dr Reid, and his quest for Utopia, will give rise to the cataclysms of the twentieth century. But for one brief, shining, "belle époque" moment, there is peace, and space for the imagination to run free.   — A.M.